Tricky Conversations

ANDREW FULLER

Tricky Conversations

How to have less conflict
and more peace in your life

Published in 2024 by Amba Press, Melbourne, Australia
www.ambapress.com.au

© Andrew Fuller 2024

All rights reserved. No part of this book may be reproduced or transmitted in any form or by any means, electronic or mechanical, including photocopying, recording or by any information storage and retrieval system, without prior permission in writing from the publisher.

First published as *Tricky People* by Finch Publishing in 2009.
Republished by HarperCollins Publishers in 2013.

Cover design: Tess McCabe
Internal design: Amba Press
Editor: Andrew Campbell

The illustration on the inside front cover and page 4 are reproduced with permission from Ray Eckermann and Independent Schools Victoria.

ISBN: 9781923215184 Print
ISBN: 9781923215191 eBook

A catalogue record for this book is available from the National Library of Australia.

Disclaimer: While every care has been taken in researching and compiling the information in this book, it is in no way intended to replace professional legal advice and counselling. Readers are encouraged to seek such help as they deem necessary. The author and publisher specifically disclaim any liability arising from the application of information in this book.

About the author

Andrew Fuller is a clinical psychologist and family therapist who specialises in resilience, brains, and learning strengths. Andrew works with schools, students, and parents across the world.

Andrew is an author of many books, including: *Guerrilla Tactics for Teachers: The Essential Classroom Management Guide*, *Neurodevelopmental Differentiation: Optimising Brain Systems for Learning*, *Your Best Life at Any Age*, *The A to Z of Feelings*, *Tricky People, Tricky Behaviours*, *Unlocking Your Child's Genius*, *Raising Real People*, *From Surviving to Thriving*, *Work Smarter Not Harder* and *Beating Bullies*.

Contents

Introduction 1

Part 1: Successfully resolving tricky conversations 5

Chapter 1   Conflict for beginners 7
Chapter 2   Identifying how you relate in tricky conversations 17
Chapter 3   Back-stabbers 27
Chapter 4   Blamers and Whingers 43
Chapter 5   Bullies and Tyrants 58
Chapter 6   Controllers and Gaslighters 74
Chapter 7   High and Mighties 94
Chapter 8   Avoiders 109
Chapter 9   Competitors 124
Chapter 10   Poor Communicators 138

Part 2: Help for everyone – including tricky people 151

Chapter 11   If the tricky person in your life is you 153
Chapter 12   Workplace politics – a survival guide 157
Chapter 13   Tricky conversations and relationship patterns 164
Chapter 14   How to make a tricky person your best teacher 179

Author's notes 185
Acknowledgements 187
References 188
Index 189

Introduction

Someone approaches you with a head full of fury and steam. They launch a diatribe in your direction that questions your integrity, the circumstances of your birth, and your intellectual capacity. As tempting as it is to retaliate with a vigorous defence of your personal attributes, your parentage, and your brain power, you resist. Leaping to your own defence in tricky conversations is rarely a successful strategy. Instead, you find yourself saying, "Let's not waste time discussing my own personal failings, how can I help you?"

Knowing how to conduct a tricky conversation can save you a lot of angst and unnecessary pain.

An innocent young man – let's place him in his early twenties – enters a pub to meet a friend. He scans the room only to be met with the glowering glare of a lug with too many drinks under his belt and too few neurons to counter them. The lug slurs and menacingly demands to know if the young man is looking at "his woman". While it is tempting to engage the inquirer in a discussion that informs him that women are not the possessions of men and therefore the description of "his woman" is factually if not morally incorrect, it is more likely to gain him a smack in the kisser than to advance the causes of feminism and humanism. Enlightening inebriated people of their ignorance and outmoded value systems is rarely a successful strategy in tricky conversations. Instead, our young man briskly replies, "I was wondering if her name is Emma? I think she went to school with my sister, Kate."

Deftly dealing with tricky people and creating diversions is a skill that once acquired not only can reduce violence, but can also soothe addled souls and increase peace in the world.

"I am not qualified to make diagnoses, but in your case…"

"Be careful before you start flinging around amateur diagnostic labels."

"You are such a narcissist!"

"The question is not whether I should take on your unqualified diagnosis, but whether you should start to believe it yourself."

The art of effectively conducting a tricky conversation is a skill that benefits everyone.

It is also a skill that everyone will need at some point of their lives. Hopefully you are one of the lucky ones – surrounded by an endless list of thoughtful, kind sweethearts who can see reason and consider a multitude of perspectives on almost any issue. If so, celebrate. However, at times you may be bailed up by people who decide that one of the best ways to offload their own collection of emotional baggage and personal poison is to vent it in your direction. It is for managing *those* people in *those* moments that this book is designed.

Early on in my career I worked in psychiatric crisis teams helping people in the darkest moments of their lives. Some of them were considering ending their lives. As green and as unprepared as I was, I already understood that just saying to them "Don't do it" wasn't going to be enough. Instead, I said, "You must be surprised that life has led you to this point. Would you mind talking about it before you decide what to do." I was very fortunate: they all agreed to talk, and thankfully, no one followed through on their initial plans.

What inspired this book?

Throughout my career, I have sat with people in therapy who have been distraught about the tricky people in their lives, and I have been a consultant to thousands of workplaces and teams where tricky conversations, or the inability to have them, have ruled the roost and inflicted pain on well-meaning colleagues. The lessons from my work have been instilled in this book.

The thousands of people I have worked with have been lovely, caring, intelligent people who have done their best to accommodate, acclimatise to, avoid or acquiesce to tricky people. But unfortunately, accommodating, acclimatising to, avoiding or acquiescing to tricky people does not work. Ever. End of story.

Knowing how to conduct a tricky conversation and to deal with tricky people is an important life skill.

This book is a composite of ideas that have been researched, tried and tested for over 35 years. Workshops conducted by myself and sometimes with my great colleague Dr Stephen Brown have revealed the power of knowing how to effectively conduct a tricky conversation. One of the questions people discuss is the trickiest conversation they ever had in their lives. One woman's reply was, "The one I was never brave enough to have."

I'm not sure of the original reason why I decided to turn my findings into a book. Maybe it was the surgical team who threw scalpels at one another when things didn't go their way during an operation. Maybe it was the corporate team who traded personal insults even though they had never actually met face to face. Perhaps it was the engineer who slammed down the phone after screaming into it, "I haven't got time to tell you who this is, just get him to call the &%*^$@ back!" Or perhaps it was the music group who couldn't sing from the same song sheet. I'm not sure, but I do know that this world needs to have more strategies to create peace than it has to make war.

A person who owns a copy of the earlier version of this book, *Tricky People*, told me, "This book is wonderful. You don't even have to read it. I take it to difficult meetings and place it on the table, and people suddenly behave in more civilised ways."

Another reader told me, "It makes a great Christmas gift for relatives – just don't underline the parts that relate to them!"

To all the tricky people I have met in my life, thank you for teaching me how to write this book.

And to all those who have found me to be a tricky person, please accept my apologies.

Note

In the interests of fairness, the use of "he" and "she" alternates when an unspecified person is referred to. More often, the generic third-person pronoun "they" is used in the singular as well as the plural.

Tricky Conversations

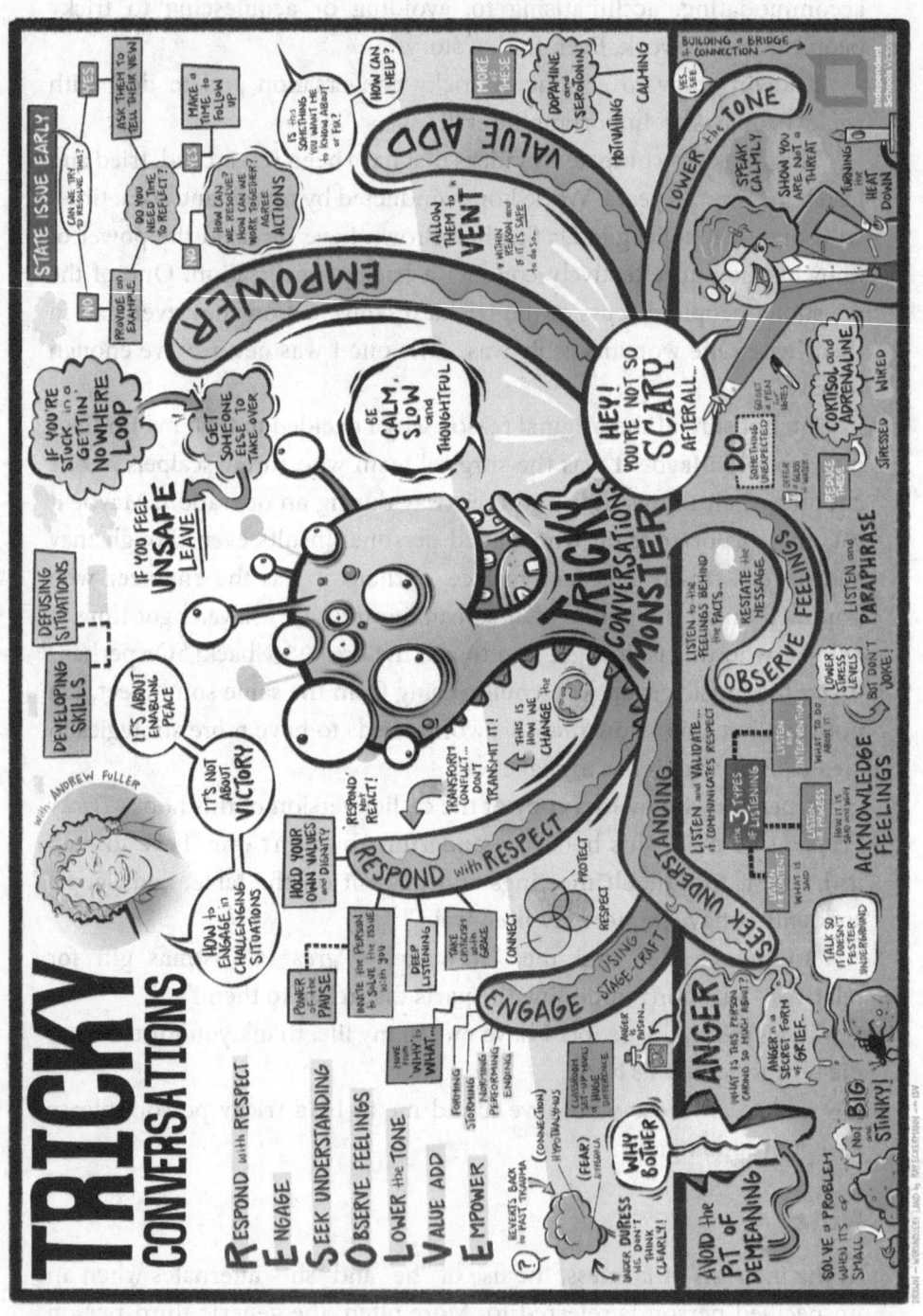

Illustrated by Ray Eckermann for Independent Schools Victoria during a professional learning event presented by Andrew Fuller.

Part 1

Successfully resolving tricky conversations

Chapter 1
Conflict for beginners

"Hell is other people."
Jean-Paul Sartre

You probably wouldn't want to sit down and have a cup of tea or a conversation with prominent figures in world history such as Genghis Khan or Attila the Hun – or even Joan of Arc, for that matter – but you'd have to admit they would be damned handy to have on your side in a scrap. In the arena of tricky conversations, when compared to these "masters of the art", you are a fledgling beginner.

Tricky people are human dynamite sticks who impact on all that goes on around them – exciting, dramatic, powerful and often a right royal pain in the rear-end. Even so, they get things done and they get people talking. When a tricky person does something, it generally stays done. Learn how to harness their skills and passions and you have a secret weapon that makes the Stealth Bomber look, well, a bit second-rate.

If you have one or more tricky people in your life, this book is for you. This is the guide book for navigating conversations with them and resolving conflicts. You may be trying to live with them, work for them, manage them (well, at least attempting to), be part of a family with them, or just co-exist with them in a semi-harmonious way that won't set off the next world war.

Whatever you are trying to do with them, this book will help you firstly identify them, and then provide you with strategies for remaining sane while being with them. It will even help you to use the energies of tricky people for your own benefit.

Tricky people are a wild, lurching mob that could at times fall under the banner of:

PEOPLE BEST AVOIDED!

However, as we all learn, they aren't that easy to avoid. Even when you leave workplaces, clubs, friendships or romances, they have an ability to show up again. Different face, maybe, but same issue.

Whether they are members of your family, friends or work colleagues, the conundrums they provide can leave you in knots if you are not very careful. They can have you twisting and turning in the middle of the night while they sleep the unperturbed sleep of the guilt-free. They can consume you with fury and toxify your life. You may well end up wailing and gnashing your teeth over their latest exploits.

This book is designed to help you navigate the intricacies of workplace politics, sidestep the intrigues of family dramas, and rise exultantly from the hotbed of rumour and innuendo. So, gird your loins, grab a stiff drink, and breathe deeply: your opponents are serious competition. They are scarily used to the world of co-conspirators, deceit, bragging, slashing and burning, and slander … Oh, and they are far better at squabbling and sniping than you are.

Most of these people, it is fair to say, do not play well as part of a team.

In this book you will learn how to **RESOLVE** tricky conversations:

- **R** Respond with respect
- **E** Engage
- **S** Seek understanding
- **O** Observe feelings
- **L** Lower the tone
- **V** Value-add
- **E** Empower

We'll look at developing these skills in work, family, romantic and social settings.

Work settings

People often report that the most stressful aspect of their job isn't time pressure or the tasks they are required to do; it's the tricky conversations they end up having with people they have to work with. The snide, snivelling ways of some colleagues not only can become depressingly familiar, they can also make you ill. Sadly, it is not only individual co-workers who hold this power; some workplaces have cultures that are toxic.

Organisations have an invasive power over the people within them. They grip and they stick. One of the oddest aspects of organisations is they often behave in ways that are precisely the reverse of their intentions in the world. This is known as their "shadow", and it often shows up as the awful and shoddy treatment of workers. It is the dark side of good intentions. And it's often the "best" organisations that have the deepest shadows.

The idea of an organisational "shadow" helps us to understand why hospital staff are often at loggerheads with one another despite providing wonderful levels of care for their patients. This also helps us to understand why mental health and social welfare agencies are often a bit mad, why bankers can become spendthrifts or gamblers, why teachers can bully and belittle one another, and why religious organisations can become places of abysmal inhumanity for their staff despite doing wonderful spiritual work in their communities.

It almost seems that the better intentioned an organisation is, the more likely it is to treat workers badly when the chips are down. It's a bit like a tree: the bigger it is and the more light it basks in, the larger its shadow will be. Of course, this means that tricky people can wield enormous sway in these workplaces.

Family settings

Families are often full of tricky conversations that have major ramifications. Families have rules about topics that can and cannot be discussed.

Families follow patterns. They do the same thing in much the same way, over and over again.

When a tricky person is also a family member, he or she has special power over us. As a result, he or she can diminish your achievements, make light of your passions, and belittle any positive changes you may have made. This is why times of family gathering are difficult for many people.

One woman told me her experience of this:

> I travelled overseas for three months' backpacking. I was tanned, fit. I'd faced my fears and grown incredibly as a person. For the first time in my life I could look at myself in the mirror and really like the person who looked back. I glowed. I returned home to see my family. You know the first thing they did? They looked at me and said, "You haven't changed a bit."

Tricky conversational skills will help you to identify the patterns and rules of family life, and to either sidestep them or use them to create healthier interactions.

Romantic settings

The complexity of tricky conversations reaches an all-time high in the world of romance. Even when all is well, conversations can turn tricky in a heartbeat. If things are a bit rocky on the romantic front, the intricacies of tricky conversations amplify dramatically. If you are sharing custody of children with an estranged former partner, the heat is turned up to full throttle.

Even if you have left your ex a long time ago, they have an interesting ability to live on, rent-free, in your mind. You can end up having tricky conversations even though your ex isn't actually there.

In new romances, tricky people are often very clear-headed, knowing exactly what they want and know how to get it. You may be placed high on a pedestal one moment, only to be ground into the dirt a moment later. If you are a person who really wants others to like you (a.k.a. "the please disease"), you are putty in their hands.

It is possible to create great and loving romances with tricky people, but this is only for those who are certain about what they want and are prepared to stand their ground to get it.

Social settings

Almost every friendship will have some difficult moments when trust is tested, and a tricky conversation may be needed to pull it through to the other side.

Friendships can be like roller coasters. Tricky friends will often have very good ideas about ways you can improve your life. Some will even insist that you adopt these. Some will teach you how to be generous by borrowing your belongings and never returning them. Others will help you learn how to be gracious when faced with the glowing success of others. Good friendship with a tricky person requires a determined self-confidence and involves some bracing moments. It may be prickly at times, but it may also be good for you.

Tricky people can teach us a lot about how life should ideally operate, and what to do when it doesn't work out that way. For example, there is a belief that if you live your life well, are nice to others, and are polite and graceful, nice things will happen to you. In the Christian tradition this sentiment is contained in ideas like "turn the other cheek" and "the meek shall inherit the earth". In the Hindu tradition it is karma; in Islam it is kismet (the concept of wishing for others what you wish for yourself); and in Judaism it is the idea of loving your neighbour as yourself.

Certainly, being pleasant and friendly is a good default position. But know clearly and firmly that some people are not going to be swayed by niceness.

Treating other people well is a great way to live life, but the world's traditions have not conspired for you to be walked all over either. Tricky people will treat you like a human doormat if you let them.

You can treat people well without being dominated by them

Most of us don't really want to have tricky conversations. Most of us wish that tricky people would go away and bother someone else. Sadly, they won't. In fact, they will come back even stronger and more determined.

Many people will do almost anything rather than sort out a relationship that has fallen into difficulty. When the other person is a formidable tricky person, most of us head for the hills rather than confront the issue directly.

Some of the common ways people ineffectively have tricky conversations is to fight, run away, or "freeze and seethe".

Fight

Trying to match someone in a tricky conversation and come out with all guns blazing is rarely a successful strategy. Firstly, he or she is much more used to scrapping and fighting than you are. Secondly, this rarely occurs when you have planned it, and often happens when you have a head full of steam. Acting on the spur of the moment is almost never a good idea with tricky people: you become an emotional and erratic loose cannon, and they can dismiss you as over-reacting, hysterical and unstable.

The first great lesson that tricky people will teach you is that solving major relationship issues takes great care and cool-headed planning.

Run away

The second big lesson is that you can run but you cannot hide from tricky conversations. The world is full of tricky people. They are your opponents, and unless you use them to learn lessons for yourself, you will repeatedly run up against the same issues or types of people.

Conversing with tricky people may not always be a lot of fun, but it can help you play better in the game of life. Avoiding them only intensifies issues. Some of them may be your worst enemies; they may also be your best teachers. Avoiding tricky people usually only amplifies your own vulnerabilities.

Freeze and seethe

Very few of us seek out tricky conversations. They terrify us. "Freeze and seethe" is our most common response. This is the "bunny in the headlights" reaction, where you do nothing but accept the toxicity the tricky person has directed at you and then take it home and lose sleep.

Even worse, you may begin to inflict some version of the toxicity on your loved ones. You may start complaining about the tricky person to people who have no power to change the behaviour of the tricky person – absolutely pointless. This book is designed to help you not do that.

MEMORABLE INSULTS

"Always back the horse named self-interest, son.
It will be the only one trying."

Jack Lang

"Thank you for sending me a copy of your book;
I'll waste no time reading it."

Moses Hadas

Overview of RESOLVE

With all tricky conversations we use the acronym RESOLVE to guide us. This is not only designed to empower you but also aims to increase the chances of peace in your world.

- **R** Respond with respect
- **E** Engage
- **S** Seek understanding
- **O** Observe feelings
- **L** Lower the tone
- **V** Value-add
- **E** Empower

Respond with respect

If we don't transform conflict, we transmit it. Conflict can consume lives and can be passed down from generation to generation. Conflict is dangerously infectious.

What transforms conflict is shifting from disconnection to connectedness. When we comprehend the human pain behind most tricky conversations, we are more immune to conversational toxicity and more able to soothe and alleviate troubles.

Thoughtful planning and preparation are always more successful than reactivity.

 Engage

You don't have to turn up to every tricky conversation you are invited to. There are some people who will invite you to many tricky conversations. Some of these invitations you may gracefully decline. Consider what your standard replies will be:

a. If you decide not to accept their invitation, say "I'm sorry you are feeling upset; I hope things improve for you" and then move away.
b. If you decide to engage in a tricky conversation, say "I can see you are feeling upset or angry; can I try to help?"

 Seek understanding

Conversations become healthy (and less tricky) when people move from certainty to curiosity, wondering what has happened to create the upset. What forms connection is true listening, with minimal interruptions. Try as much as possible to understand the situation and how the other person views it.

Even when you don't share values with the other person, try to identify shared interests or objectives.

 Observe feelings

Thoughts and feelings occur in waves. When people are upset, there are often peaks and troughs in their intensity. Conversational interventions timed during the calmer intervals in a conversation are more likely to be successful.

Anger often indicates what people care deeply about. People build fortresses to protect themselves from the ferocity of their own anger. Gaining a sense of the issue that is behind the wall of anger helps to resolve it.

 Lower the tone

Soothing a tricky conversation so that the issue becomes solvable involves lowering the stress hormones (cortisol and adrenaline) and increasing those associated with bonding and connection (oxytocin, vasopressin and dopamine).

 Value-add

Adding value to a tricky conversation involves considering the answer to "What is missing that if you had it would make this problem be over?"

 Empower

The successful outcome of a tricky conversation does not necessarily involve you calming and agreeing with the other person. It usually requires feeling heard and obtaining a fair and just solution. The aim of tricky conversations is not for you to calm the other person but for them to calm themselves.

Map for tricky conversations

R Respond with respect
- [ ] Do I need to respond at all? What will happen if I do nothing?
- [ ] Conduct a power-base analysis (see Chapter 2).
- [ ] Can I intervene effectively?
- [ ] If you decide that you should respond, and your intervention is likely to be worthwhile, pause and prepare yourself. Ask yourself:
  - "What is the outcome I am hoping to achieve?"
  - "Is this conversation worth having?"
  - "If I only got 50% of the outcome I am looking for, what would that look like? Could I be OK with that?"
- [ ] Be calm.
- [ ] Develop curiosity or even fascination.

E Engage
- [ ] State the issue early.
- [ ] Ask: "Can we try to resolve this?"
- [ ] Ask: "Are you aware of the situation?"

S Seek understanding
- [ ] If no, provide an example.
- [ ] If yes, ask: "Can you tell me your view of it?"

O Observe feelings
- [ ] Be aware of your emotional responses.
- [ ] Do not feel you need to share your feelings.
- [ ] Ask: "Do you need time to reflect on this?"

L Lower the tone
- [ ] Reassure

V Value-add
- [ ] Ask: "How can we resolve this?"
- [ ] Ask: "How can we work together on this?"
- [ ] Ask: "What help from me would be helpful?"
- [ ] Ask: "What is missing that if you had it would make this problem be over?"

E Empower
- [ ] Agree on actions.
- [ ] Agree to follow up to review.
- [ ] Conduct a personal review – what can I learn from this for the future?

Chapter 2
Identifying how you relate in tricky conversations

"Any man who tries to be good all the time is bound to come to ruin among the great number who are not good."

Niccoló Machiavelli

Welcome to the world of trickiness!

The first thing we need to know in order to start dealing with tricky conversations more effectively is how we usually handle or cope with them.

"Whenever conflict appears, I go to water. My knees tremble, my voice dries up, I can't think, and my only desire is to get out of there as quickly as possible."

"Well, if we have to have an argument, let's get it out in the open and over and done with. I don't have time to spend worrying about tricky people – I've got a life to lead here."

"People don't really know me or understand me. They see me as flighty and lightweight, a real airhead. That lets them feel they can take me for granted, and that I won't get too upset if they change plans on me. Actually I go home and silently plot all types of revenge."

"I'm a worrier. If there is ever any flare-up with someone, I spend the rest of the day raking over the coals, turning each detail over and over in my mind. I sleep with gritted teeth."

Do any of these patterns sound familiar? We all have our own individual style of relating in tricky conversations. Some of us try to charge through like a water buffalo stung by a bee, others try to plea-bargain to a higher court, others meticulously and obsessively sift through the details, while yet others blame themselves and try to appease the other person.

The tables on the next few pages will help you to work out the strengths and vulnerabilities of your own style.

Please circle one answer for each statement. One way of answering this is to consider which of the four options is easiest or comes most naturally for you.

Strengths and vulnerabilities

A	B	C	D
1. I am best at:			
Making realistic decisions	Reaching accurate conclusions	Uncovering hidden connections	Understanding people's feelings
2. I am happiest when my environment is:			
Busy	Safe and secure	Friendly	Task-oriented
3. I learn best by:			
Experimenting and tinkering	Listening and sharing	"Hunching" and exploring	Reflecting and thinking
4. Most people would identify me as:			
Productive	Creative	Responsive	Logical
5. One of my strengths is:			
Planning	Enthusiasm	Practicality	Listening
6. When learning something new, I enjoy:			
Exploring hidden possibilities	Organising ideas	Making personal connections	Producing results
7. I strive for:			
Agreement	Precision	Efficiency	Adventure
8. Generally I am:			
Nurturing	Precise	Decisive	Intuitive

Identifying how you relate in tricky conversations

A	B	C	D
9. If anything, I tend to be:			
Too impulsive	Too sensitive	To action-oriented	Too critical
10. Generally I am:			
Cooperative	Orderly	Straightforward	Free-spirited
11. When I don't know an answer for something, I tend to:			
Get on with the task even though I haven't got the answer	Ask for more information about the task	Seek reassurance or ask others	Move on to something else and forget about it
12. I am most comfortable with people who are:			
Supportive	Innovative	Productive	Rational
13. I am least comfortable with people who are:			
Inflexible	Disorganised	Indecisive	Aggressive
14. Generally I am:			
Studious	People-oriented	Down to earth	Innovative
15. If given a choice, I would probably prefer to:			
Make the world a happier place	Learn new facts	Solve practical problems	Create new ways of doing things

Discovering your style

Use the scoring key below to code your answers in the table above.

	A	B	C	D		A	B	C	D
1	W	WO	V	H	9	V	H	W	WO
2	V	WO	H	W	10	H	WO	W	V
3	V	H	W	WO	11	W	WO	W	V
4	W	V	H	WO	12	H	V	H	WO
5	WO	V	W	H	13	V	WO	W	H
6	V	WO	H	W	14	WO	H	W	V
7	H	WO	W	V	15	H	WO	W	V
8	H	WO	W	V					

Now count up the total numbers of:

W (Warrior) _____
V (Visionary) _____
H (Healer) _____
WO (Wise One) _____

to determine your main style.

Warrior

Congratulations! You tend to be a gung-ho, take-no-prisoners, get-on-with-it type of person. The unconscious belief that you often operate from is that you have to compete or you will be under attack.

Strengths	Vulnerabilities	To work on or watch out for
Action-oriented. Just do it. Not reliant on advice from others.	Not enough thinking time. You don't sit down and talk. May not seek out or have the support of others.	Preparing your strategies. Ask others for input and advice – this also builds allies.
Decisive.	Impulsive.	Being too eager to get to a solution.
You write lists and tick things off – and achieve a lot.	People can feel railroaded and not listened to.	Realise others take more time to chat about and consider matters than you do.
You look for an outcome as soon as possible.	Can come up with "narrow" solutions to problems.	Ask other creative people what they would do.
Once a problem is solved, you move on.	Can fail to consider the fall-out or longer-term implications of a problem.	Get in the practice of going back to people and checking that the problem or issue is really solved, and that they are happy to move on.
Well-intentioned.	People may not see this or may feel patronised.	Ask people how you can work with them to create the outcomes they would like.
You push for a result.	May not foresee unintended consequences.	Listening.

Visionary

Congratulations! You are an imaginative, lively, creative person with a love of big, bright, new ideas. The unconscious belief that you often operate from is that you are different from other people and that generally the rules don't apply to you.

Strengths	Vulnerabilities	To work on or watch out for
You dream up big ideas quickly and fall in love with them.	You don't always consider the details or implications for all involved.	Realise that caution on the part of others is not always an opportunity to sell your ideas more powerfully. It can be a time for listening to their concerns.
Passionate.	You can get swept up with your own ideas.	Slow down, learn to look at problems from multiple perspectives. Learn to ask yourself: "What would the most cautious person I know say about this?"
You like change (sometimes for its own sake).	You get bored easily and can feel frustrated that others are slow to catch on.	Remember that when we all take off together we become a more powerful force. Faster change is not better than change where everyone is on board.
You can imagine a world where everyone is happy.	You assume everyone will go along with an idea once they understand it clearly.	Don't spend too long persuading – it can end up feeling like cajoling. Take more time to think before starting a tricky conversation.

Healer

Congratulations! You are a warm and friendly person who is perceived by others as a good listener. The unconscious belief you often operate from is that you may get hurt by people, and that you should avoid this.

Strengths	Vulnerabilities	To work on or watch out for
You minimise conflict and maximise consensus.	Can avoid conflict to an incredible extent. May feel unhappy when people can't agree. Overly agreeable.	Avoiding conflict usually means you take it home and worry. Know that people can "agree to disagree". If you say "yes" when you really mean "no", this can lead to bitterness in the long term.
Able to see things from others' perspectives.	Can feel paralysed and anxious if there are many differing opinions.	Don't solve problems through personal sacrifice. Allocate a set amount of time for thinking about a problem, and then move on. Don't ruminate.
You look for solutions that work for everyone.	Conflicts may be unintentionally extended and go on for too long. May be overly timid.	Sometimes a quick decision that not everyone is happy with is healthier than a slow decision that everyone is still not happy with.
You take responsibility.	Can blame yourself if conflict occurs, and can put up with toxic tricky people for too long.	There is no great virtue in self-blame. Put your energies into solving the problem.
Informed – you always knows the gossip.	Your time can be taken up by listening to others.	For every moment you spend hearing what others want, spend some time thinking about what you want.

Wise One

Congratulations! You are thoughtful, seeking ideas and being thorough before reaching a solution. The unconscious belief that you often operate from is that you should be in control, and that if you have enough information you will know how to control any situation.

Strengths	Vulnerabilities	To work on or watch out for
You consider a wide range of possibilities.	Can spend long periods of time preparing to work with tricky people.	Be careful that events aren't moving faster than your planning, so you get left behind.
You seek out knowledge and perspectives before coming to a position.	Can be seen as ponderous and slow by others.	Don't suffer from "analysis paralysis". Plan, but set a time for action.
You know that the process of reaching a decision can be as important as the outcome.	Your own thoroughness can at times blind you to your power and creativity.	Be prepared to share your ideas. They will often be better thought-out than those of others.
You want to solve conflict through logic.	May disregard the emotional nature of conflict.	Don't be dismissive of people in highly emotional states. Listen to them, but hold fire on your solutions until later.
You perceptively absorb vast amounts of information.	Hesitancy.	Use information, but gather only enough to guide action. Be bold.

Let's meet these tricky people

Tricky conversations invariably involve someone who is difficult to manage, relate to, negotiate with, live with, or just plain put up with.

In the following pages you will read descriptions of common tricky people and the conversations that can twist you into knots.

The bewildering array of underhand, manipulative, and sometimes just plain nasty behaviours can leave you with the blurred sense that your tricky person fits into all of the categories. Fear not, dear reader, for these behaviours occur in clusters. Your tricky person may well span one or two categories. The main issue here is to help you identify the key areas that plague you, and to then help you work out a course of action.

This is a crash course in identifying tricky people in your friendship group, family, workplace and romantic life.

One of the most common errors people make in relationships is assuming that the other person is similar to them. Often this is not so.

Tricky people can be quite distinctive, and being aware of their ways helps you plan how to cope with them.

A quick look at who you are dealing with

Please choose the behaviours that your tricky person exhibits:

1. Spreads rumours and bad news about you
2. Tries to make himself look good at others' expense
3. Always complains
4. Acts like it's always somebody else's fault
5. Puts you down
6. Is nasty and mean
7. Doesn't pass on important information
8. Has to always have it done his way – no one else ever has any good ideas
9. Makes you feel worthless
10. Always claims to be superior
11. Is hard to pin down; is as slippery as an eel
12. Promises the world, delivers little
13. Argues the point over petty things
14. Can't stand to lose at anything
15. Goes off the handle without provocation
16. Says really stupid things.

If you chose 1–4, you have a sneaky tricky person in your life. Read Chapter 3 on Back-stabbers and Chapter 4 on Blamers and Whingers.

If you chose 5–8, you have a dominating person on your hands. Read Chapter 5 on Bullies and Tyrants and Chapter 6 on Controllers and Gaslighters.

If you chose 9–12, you have a snooty tricky person on your hands. Read Chapter 7 on High and Mighties and Chapter 8 on Avoiders.

If you chose 13–16, you have a compulsive and repulsive tricky person in your world. Read Chapter 9 on Competitors and Chapter 10 on Poor Communicators.

If you chose them all, you had best read the whole book!

Before a tricky conversation do this first!

Analysing power bases – yours and theirs

Before you do anything, do this. Embarking on a tricky conversation takes planning. Importantly, you need to determine if having the conversation is worth having and whether you have any chance at all of improving the situation.

Complete the analysis to assess the relative power between you and your tricky person. The balance of power between the two of you can help you decide whether to act directly, bide your time and gather resources, or give up and head for the hills.

For each of the following issues, rate yourself and your tricky person out of 10 (1 = hopeless; 10 = fantastic). Then add these up to obtain a total for him and for you.

Personal resources	Their rating	Your rating
Ability to change or be flexible		
Ability to express your thoughts and feelings clearly		
Self-confidence		
Confidence in own viewpoint		
Past ability to deal with conflict		
Ability to see things clearly and to decide with a cool head		
Ability to see the situation from the other person's perspective		
Ability to be assertive		
External resources	**Their rating**	**Your rating**
Reputation		
Abilities that are hard to replace		
Position		
Level of information (has all the facts)		
Level of support from powerful others		

Results

If you are well ahead on points, consider direct forms of action such as confrontation and direct discussion. If you are only slightly ahead, delay, and plan to build your power base. Go hunting for allies.

If the tricky person has more points, be aware of his strength. Use indirect methods at best or stop trying to challenge him. Build barricades to protect yourself from his toxicity.

But before you do anything – including deciding to act – take some time to reflect on the following questions:

- What would your/their best supporter say about this?
- What would your/their worst enemy say about this?
- What will you do if the outcome doesn't go your way?

Chapter 3

Back-stabbers

"If you haven't got anything nice to say about anybody, come sit next to me."

Alice Roosevelt Longworth

When you can fake sincerity, you can fake anything. Back-stabbers are masters and mistresses of looking as sweet as pie in front of you, but turn your back and you are easy pickings. This group contains connivers, plotters, fakers, rumour-mongers, show ponies, gossips, crawlers and big talkers – and that's just the most likeable of them!

Great Back-stabbers of history

- Brutus
- Judas
- Lady Macbeth
- Mark Antony – swept Cleopatra away from Caesar and then took his empire
- Iago – whispered nasty things about Desdemona into Othello's ear.

How to spot Back-stabbers

Back-stabbers live by several rules:

- Rule 1: look good.
- Rule 2: avoid looking bad.
- Rule 3: if you can look good and have others look bad, even better.

They strengthen their own sense of self by talking about other people's inadequacies. This is common when romances and marriages break up. In fact it almost seems like many people are unable to separate from one another without having to justify it.

Diagnostic checklist for Back-stabbers
- Brag and boast
- Claim contributions or achievements as their own that are not theirs
- Hoard information
- Are happy to spread negative news about others
- Smooch and cruise
- Spread gossip
- Claim credit for things they didn't do
- Appear to have more contacts and connections to powerful people than is the case
- Are selective about whom they praise or talk to
- Are undermining
- Often conceal feelings of inadequacy and fearfulness.

Favourite phrases
- "Unfortunately [x] wasn't able to help in this project as much as I'm sure she would have liked to …"
- "Well, he's good friend … most of the time."
- "She's as sweet as pie when she wants something."
- "I'm sure he loves people … almost as much as he loves himself."

The goal of their behaviour

Gaining personal advantage or satisfaction at the expense of others is their aim.

Key strategies
- They are masters and mistresses of innuendo, rumour and the back-handed compliment.
- Using a raised eyebrow, a roll of an eye, or a sly grimace, a seemingly innocent or positive comment is converted into a poisoned arrow.

- They are accomplished at talking in double meanings, where the surface meaning is one thing but the intended meaning is quite another.

In the workplace

At work, these flash-in-the-pan show ponies will exaggerate their own accomplishments while minimising yours. They are not on your side. You may find yourself fading into invisibility in comparison with their self-portrayed magnificence.

According to them, they have put in the hard yards, sweated and toiled, and generated inspirational ideas while you idled and frittered away the time.

Accomplished at greasing up leaders, they can smooch and cruise with aplomb. They are adept at covering up their own tracks while shining a searchlight on your innocent but wayward footprints.

If you are working with them, know that Back-stabbers delight when others are in hot water, so gather the ice cubes and grab your swimming gear – you could be in a spot of bother. Collaboration and cooperation are not the strongest points of any of the tricky people described in this book, and this is particularly true for Back-stabbers.

Some people you know will back you up, uphold your reputation, and defend your integrity. These, my friends, aren't them. View them as your own negative public-relations officers, and you won't go far wrong. They are happy to spread news of your latest foible or broadcast any mistakes you've ever made – with colleagues like these you won't need enemies. If they are clever, they will avoid big complaints and focus on drip-feeding niggling issues about you.

Confide your secrets or worries to them, and they will blab to the world. They sing like canaries in a choir.

Some of the methods used by Back-stabbers in organisations include the following.

Restricting the supply of information to you

Knowledge is power, but even better for Back-stabbers is having knowledge and depriving others of information. This allows them to look informed and you to look out of date and inept. They may even watch you working hard on a project, only to later "sympathetically" ask you, "Didn't you get the message that this has been cancelled?"

These destructive time-wasters will withhold information about meetings, fail to pass on phone messages, forget to pass on invitations, fail to mention changed timelines – anything to get an edge over you. You can end up feeling used, bruised and accused.

Feigning support and empathy

An example of this would be a Back-stabber saying to your mutual colleagues, "It's such a shame [your name] put so much work into that paper, and the manager still wants it improved."

Other ways of doing this include:

- "He's had a lot on lately, so we shouldn't expect too much."
- "Perhaps it's that time of the month …"
- "I'm worried about [your name]. I think you're overloading them with work [or they are looking tired]. Can I do anything to help?"

Increasing their visibility and your invisibility

Back-stabbers usually love being noticed. You'll find them up the front in any staff or family photos. They attend events to be seen and to further their career. They would go to the opening of an envelope.

If you are managing or leading them, be afraid, very afraid. Your reputation could slip down the plug-hole of life very easily. Their ambition contains ruthlessness. If your team contains some snide Back-stabbers, rumours are your enemy and documented facts are your friends.

Basically, there are three types of employee in a workplace – cats, dogs and rats:

- The cats are loyal to the place. In fact, they think they own the place.
- The dogs are loyal to the team. They wag their tails and follow people around.
- The rats are just loyal to themselves. There is nothing wrong with being a rat – you just need to know if you are one.

Back-stabbers are, without exception, rats. They will play to the highest bidder, and their loyalty is written in water.

Back-stabbers are all too happy to share the dirt on others. Shrewd managers can use them to find out all sorts of information. In some circumstances you may be able to trade information for loyalty. For example, say to them, "I will back you up on this, but first I need a bit of information on …"

However, never forget that these are people who make slippery agreements. You may get the impression that they have agreed to a course of action, only to hear later that they have said, "Well, I wouldn't have done it that way."

If one is your boss, the likely reason she is your boss is because she has learned to suppress potential competitors for her position through strong disinformation campaigns. And she is not going to give up this strategy lightly. Back-stabbers resemble dictators who, upon gaining power, have all the other bright leaders in the country rounded up and shot. They are like politicians who, after gaining power, send their brightest colleagues off to become ambassadors in obscure places like Upper Volograd North.

Not wanting to trouble you

In this situation Back-stabbers delay informing you of an issue until it builds into a major setback. Under the guise of not wanting to trouble you, they will feign ignorance of the negative potential of a situation or event and fail to give you advance warning until it is too late to be avoided. The person who is at fault is not them (they were just an innocent bystander).

Have a no-surprises policy in your workplace. We know there will be times when things don't work out. However, I need to know before the media get in touch with me.

In your personal and social life

These two-faced snitches can be hard to handle socially. Essentially, you can't trust them as far as you could spit a rat. These sickly-sweet Back-stabbers will cheerily welcome you, then use any opportunity to undermine you. And just because they make you feel a bit paranoid doesn't mean they are not out to get you.

It is possible to maintain a friendship with these tricky people, but you have to know whom you are dealing with. You can swim with sharks and not get nipped, but you need a lot of protection to do so.

With Back-stabbers, you need to be prepared for your contributions to be largely overlooked. As Harry Truman once commented, "You can achieve anything as long as you don't mind who gets the credit." Back-stabbers clamour for attention and praise. To be friends with them, be prepared to provide a lot of both.

Back-stabbers and romance

Romantically, be careful. Falling in love with them is a dicey proposition. Dinner conversations are likely to follow the pattern of "That's enough about you; let's talk about me". Back-stabbers can be alluringly seductive as they dazzle you with their exploits and accomplishments. They can make it appear that they have achieved wonders despite often being surrounded by a mediocre, talentless mob. Hear the warning bell: one day that "mediocre, talentless mob" may well include you. Of course, Back-stabbers can experience genuine love. Often they form intense relationships that can resemble a conspiratorial coven. "It's us against the world" may be their love motto. They find unity in adversity.

Back-stabbers can be amusing and thoughtful lovers if you treat your relationship like an exclusive club that very few are bright enough or talented enough to enter. But if falling in love with them can be dicey, falling out of love can be truly dangerous. Having spent years back-stabbing others, they may direct all of these talents at you. In some cases they run off with your best friend. In the process they may share information about your sexual proclivities, the inadequacy of your body parts, or your resonant snoring after a long day.

A few years ago, a woman sent a lovely email to her new man attesting to his prowess as a lover and recounting in vivid detail their activities of the previous evening, their first encounter. In an act of treachery he posted the email, including the woman's name and email address, on the internet.

Unfortunately, anything can be used against you once the Back-stabber has fallen out of love with you. Letters, photos, home movies, and personal information can all be posted on social media for the world to see. So brace yourself – storm clouds are accumulating. Of course, wise advice would be to never share personal information with potentially back-stabbing lovers. But then again, what would love be if it weren't a little bit silly?

Tricky conversations with Back-stabbers

With all tricky conversations we use the acronym RESOLVE to guide us. This is not only designed to empower you but also aims to increase the chances of peace in your world.

- **R** Respond with respect
- **E** Engage
- **S** Seek understanding
- **O** Observe feelings
- **L** Lower the tone
- **V** Value-add
- **E** Empower

R Respond with respect

Being able to overcome the initial impulse to react to whatever the Back-stabber has done is the first step towards managing this effectively. Crafting a response takes some time and some thought, but it is worthwhile.

The first consideration is whether any response is:

a. Called for
b. Likely to be effective.

For this reason, we always begin with the power base analysis in Chapter 2.

In sports, opponents are easily recognised by the colour of their uniform. In real life, the opposition is harder to pick.

With tricky people, it is really important to not just listen to their words. They are adept at concealing their true intentions. Kind words can mask treacherous acts. Instead, it is important to watch what they do. The way tricky people behave is a much better guide to their future actions than their words are.

Consider the consequences of allowing a Back-stabber to continue. Rumours spread; whispers accumulate. Bad news travels fast. Your reputation will be in tatters; you may be overlooked for promotion. Your friendship group or neighbourhood may shun you. Your family may look upon you as the black sheep or the wayward son or daughter. No, the answer is clear: you are going to have to act.

> *"A modest little person, with much to be modest about …"*
> Winston Churchill

Spreading rumours has become an entirely new ball game with the ability to post information on social media. These days bad news is turbo-charged with a healthy tail wind.

Gore Vidal once commented that whenever he heard that a friend of his had become successful, a little part of him died. Gore precisely pointed to the basis of most rumours: envy. Rumours can be vicious and enormously destructive. They can vary from blunt remarks ("Did you know she has had a bit of work done?") to insinuations ("He's very interested in children – almost too interested").

These are dirty games indeed. Sowing doubt is a powerful weapon. Some rumours need to be confronted. It is useful to ask yourself, "How much is my reputation worth?"

Take the time to clear your head of the thoughts that have plagued you about the tricky person. Intense interactions with tricky people can get your mind in a whirl, like a washing machine on spin cycle.

The power of tricky people's behaviour can be so intense that you can heap rage upon rage until you are so upset you've almost lost sight of what made you angry in the first place. You may even stoop to their level and start engaging in shabby behaviours. Anger is dangerous because it makes you lose perspective. Lashing out in retaliation is usually not a pretty sight; doing so without thinking it through can bring negative outcomes.

So, spring-clean your brain first. Sitting down and writing out all the thoughts, ideas, complaints and gripes you have about the Back-stabber starts this process. If you can't write them out, speak them into a recording device. Ideally, start your story with the words, "Once upon a time". Shaping your tale as if it was a children's fairytale allows you to read it over and over again, hopefully giving you some emotional distance from the tricky events.

You may initially write a long, tragic tale of demonry and despair, and then refine it down to the key actions that have taken place. Intense interactions can make us give meaning to events that have no meaning. For example, you may have thought that the Back-stabber was singling you out for special treatment, when in reality she was equally obnoxious to everyone.

Getting clear-headed is helped by exercise. You don't have to become a gym-junkie; just going for a walk regularly will do it. You've been stressed by having to put up with the tricky person, and you need some time and space to recover.

The reason that you are worrying about this situation is that you care. You care about your job, or your family, or your reputation, or your self-regard. It is now time to care for yourself as if you were your own best friend. Take some time to get out into the fresh air and walk.

> *"Ah, it's time for us to meet our maker – in my case, God, in your case, God knows. God is supposed to have made man in his own image. It would be a great shock to Christians everywhere if God looked anything like you, Baldrick."*
>
> Blackadder, to his sidekick

The thoughts and worries that beset you about tricky people can interfere with sleep. Some of us lie awake turning thoughts over and over in our minds. Others sleep the longer-than-usual hours of the exhausted and the despairing. Get sleep back into balance, somewhere between seven and nine hours a night. Sleep is probably the most powerful stress-reducer we know of.

Another important part of preparing for a response is to clearly consider if you have contributed to the current situation. This requires a tough self-examination but will help you not to repeat any mistakes of the past.

What have you done in the past when people have badmouthed you? Sat silently gritting your teeth? Brought a missile launcher to a fisticuffs battle? It is likely that your reactions have been mostly automatic and not completely thought through. As a result, the outcomes may have been a bit hit-and-miss.

This is the dilemma: to try to bolster your reputation but not look like a self-promoter. One of the great lessons Back-stabbers will help you to learn is that if you aren't prepared to build and spread some good news about yourself, you can't expect anyone else to do it for you.

> *"No one can make you feel inferior without your consent."*
> Eleanor Roosevelt

In the film *Annie Hall*, a man goes to a psychiatrist and says his wife thinks she is a hen. When the psychiatrist asks why he doesn't leave her, he says, "I can't do without the eggs."

With all types of tricky people, we need to examine whether we are collecting eggs from the situation. If we are in some way benefiting from the situation, we may need to change our own behaviour first.

With Back-stabbers, it is useful to ask yourself:

- "Have I been too compliant with this person?"
- "Have I put up with too much?"
- "Have I been too passive and allowed them to dictate my image to others?"
- "Have I been too open and trusting?"

If the answer to any of these is "yes", it doesn't mean you should assume their actions are your fault. It does mean you should take stock and consider how to change your contribution to the problem –and get on with solving it.

Your behaviour will be influenced by your way of dealing with tricky people. As mentioned previously, Warriors tend to be gung-ho, get-on-with-it types; Visionaries are creative and averse to details; Healers are people-pleasers and conflict-avoiders; and Wise Ones may be cautious and slow to act.

Based on your analysis in Chapter 2, Warriors may be tempted to confront the Back-stabber without fully thinking it through. Take time to slowly consider and plan your response.

Visionaries may feel perplexed, unfairly treated, and misunderstood. Their hurt may not come from the Back-stabber's actions, but from the willingness of other people to believe them. See the hints for dealing with hurt feelings in Chapter 13.

Healers may be tempted to blame themselves and take it personally. This can lead them to feel unable to act.

Wise Ones may want to analyse the situation over and over again in meticulous detail. This can lead to ruminating, losing sleep, and delaying necessary actions.

While this level of consideration will initially seem ponderous, over time you will become much more accomplished at manoeuvring your way through tricky conversations with Back-stabbers.

 Engage

OK, it's time to dance with the devil.

In all tricky conversations it is a good idea to shift early on from certainty to curiosity. Curiosity will resolve more tricky conversations than confrontation ever will. In the privacy of your own head you might shift from mere curiosity to total fascination at the enormity of the personality defects that this particular person appears to possess.

One technique that works well is to rattle their cage. Back-stabbers work in the murky world of sneaky subterfuge. Calling them out into the clear, cold light rattles their cages.

Organise a private discussion with a Back-stabber. Say: "I've been hearing you may have a problem with some of the things I've been doing. I'd like to hear about it directly from you."

Then pause. Let the silence become uncomfortable if need be. Silence never killed anyone, and it won't kill you.

Most Back-stabbers will deny categorically that they have had any problems with you. If this is the case, hold their gaze firmly and say: "I'm so pleased to hear that. I was really worried, and I would have been so disappointed, given our good relationship, if that had happened."

In the nicest possible way, you have signalled to the Back-stabber that you are onto them.

If they ask you who has given you this information, it's best to say: "I'd prefer to keep my sources private at this time." There is no point getting someone else into trouble or giving away your own power.

After you have left the Back-stabber's presence, document your discussion and keep a keen ear out for any rumours or complaints about you.

Sometimes just notifying a Back-stabber that you are onto them is enough to have them desist. With others, though, you may have to do more.

Assume that some of the rumours and "bad" news will have travelled. Ask a few trusted allies to speak positively about you if they hear people maligning you. Say: "There have been some false bits of information being spread around about me. As someone I have always respected, could I ask a favour of you? If you hear people speaking negatively about me, would you mind saying something positive in my defence?"

The inclination of most people is not to interfere, so unless you explicitly request people you trust to back you up, they may not see it as their role.

If necessary, prepare to correct false information yourself.

In most tricky conversations we aim for minimal but effective intervention. It is not your job to teach tricky people, and you are not the avenging angel. Use your energy for regaining your life, not for payback. Don't get into the vengeance business. Feuds are for fools. Do what you have to do and then get on with your life.

S Seek understanding

It is unlikely that you have the gift of reading other people's minds, so the actions of Back-stabbers will remain partly a mystery. Nevertheless, there are a few common threads that are likely:

- Responsibility avoidance – they point out faults in others to avoid being responsible themselves.
- Difficulties with pleasure – most of their pleasure comes at someone else's expense. This may have its origins in their childhood relationships with their siblings.

- Often avoidant – rather than dealing with concerns personally, they prefer to avoid closeness and instead snipe at others.

The best outcome you can hope for with a Back-stabber is to have your reputation intact and the enmity over. If you can, help them to be direct and consultative. Ideally, the Back-stabber will realise, at least in relation to you, that they need to be direct. When it comes to dealing with you, they will have learned not to tittle-tattle.

Know when you have got what you wanted. Tricky people can be so distracting that you can forget about the outcome you want. I have seen many people confront someone, and even though the tricky person has agreed to change their ways, the ranting continues.

Specify the outcome you are looking for and, once you've attained it, move on. This means dropping your own feelings of hostility or anger and being clearly prepared to forge a more positive relationship with the tricky person.

Observe feelings

There will be a "squirm" element to this tricky conversation. Alluding to unpleasantries and dragging them into the light of day is never comfortable.

The best way to change Back-stabbers is to be direct, up close, and personal. Have a clear intention to create a relationship that has dignity and mutual respect.

Be prepared to call out Back-stabbers on their conduct and keep calling them out on this until their actions have changed and the air between you is clear.

Back-stabbers shy away from direct approaches. The only group that exceeds them in this is the Avoiders, whom we will discuss later.

Make a decision to act rather than avoid or delay. Holding off intervening with a Back-stabber just gives them more time to spread their nasty news about you.

Be clear, direct and firm. If you have already been reassured by a Back-stabber that it wasn't them, but then discover that their ways have not changed, be blunt. Don't ask, tell. Say something like: "I now know for certain that you have been complaining about me behind my back. I would like you to stop this and deal with any issues you have with me directly with me. If I hear that you continue to do this, I will take steps to make sure you work with me in a more professional manner in the future."

Your voice may tremble as you say it. Trembling is no crime. Sound as strong as you can and, when you have said your bit, leave the scene calmly but quickly.

The car-park committee

A school I worked with had a group of parents who met every morning after dropping their children off to discuss the shortcoming of the teachers, the principal, or the school's approach to matters. This group became very powerful as stories and rumours spread – it was clear something had to be done. One of the staff members was asked to take on the role of following up each and every rumour. For several hours a day she would call the key members of this group and ask, "I hear you have some concerns about our school. Would you like to tell me what they are?" Very rarely would the Back-stabbers agree that they did have concerns. Instead, they would usually say something like, "No, no, it wasn't me. It was Mr Green who was worried."

The follow-up officer would then phone Mr Green and ask the same question.

It took six weeks of following up each and every rumour before the group was silenced.

L Lower the tone

Even if you think their assurances and pleas of innocence are about as believable as a dodgy politician's promises at election time, act as if you believe them.

The tricky conversation will contain some tension (after all, you are gently calling them to account for their actions), and indeed it requires some tension to be successful. If you are not accustomed to directly standing up for yourself (and many of us are not), you may be tempted to question yourself. "Was I too mean? Was I unfairly accusing them?" Check with a friend if you need to, and know that just going through the process of asking yourself these types of questions helps prevent trickiness in yourself. Tricky people rarely consider it necessary to reflect and conduct a self-examination of their actions.

After a tricky conversation, move on. Congratulate yourself on directly confronting a toxic issue – this is no minor accomplishment.

 Value-add

Now put your energies into marketing the "new" you. Make sure people see positive aspects of your behaviour. Become a news-maker rather than just a news-taker. This is not the time to be a shrinking violet. If you have a diverse group of colleagues, friends or family members, list their names in categories according to who believes the bad news about you completely, who is suspicious about you but is unsure, and who is clearly on your side.

Counter-marketing yourself after a period of back-stabbing may take time. Allow yourself six weeks to mount a campaign, marketing yourself as someone who is steady, calm, confident and friendly. Bolster your relationships with those who are on your side by increasing your amount of positive involvement with them.

The uncertain but wary group may also be influenced in this way. Be friendly and exemplary in a way that will allow seeds of doubt about the Back-stabber to grow. In extreme circumstances, you could consider gently nourishing any such seeds of doubt. For example, "I've been worried about [x] lately. They have seemed a bit anxious and negative. Have you noticed anything?"

 Empower

One of the reasons you have been vulnerable to Back-stabbers is that you expect that people will deal with you fairly. Inadvertently this has led you to allow cruel and malicious gossip to occur behind your back. It has also caused you to underestimate the degree of marketing you need to do to keep a positive image in the presence of flak spread by others.

Back-stabbers will teach you that:

- Your image is something you control.
- Jealousy and envy know no bounds.
- You can engage in marketing campaigns about yourself.

- If need be, you can develop a gentle counter-campaign.
- Most of all, you can be direct.

The other lesson Back-stabbers have for you is that you should develop a personal code of conduct and stick to it. This may look something like:

- No interrupting, name-calling or intimidation.
- Contribute and listen.
- Be prepared to be part of the solution.
- Express appreciation.
- Shelve it and solve it in a safe location.

Action steps: Back-stabbers

What do Back-stabbers want?	How should I respond?
To conceal feelings of anxiety	Try to increase their level of confidence so they don't need to do this
To build their self-esteem at your expense	Build allies
To build their reputation at your expense	Use counter-marketing
To promote furtive rumour-mongering	<ul><li>Be direct</li><li>Correct any misinformation</li><li>Ask direct questions</li><li>Hold them accountable</li><li>Follow up, and keep following up until they stop</li><li>Forge a positive relationship</li></ul>

MEMORABLE INSULTS

"I've just learned about his illness. Let's hope it's nothing trivial."
Irvin S. Cobb

"He is not only dull himself; he is the cause of dullness in others."
Samuel Johnson

"I didn't attend the funeral, but I sent a nice letter saying I approved of it."
Mark Twain

Chapter 4
Blamers and Whingers

*"She not only expects the worst,
but makes the worst of it when it happens."*

Michael Arlen

There is an old story about a monk who joins a monastery that observes silent prayer and reflection. Each monk is only allowed to speak two words each year. At the end of the first year, the monk comes before the head of the monastery and is told he can speak. He says, "More blankets."

Another year goes by, and the monk is called by the head and again told he can speak. The monk says, "More food."

After a third year passes, he again speaks to the head but this time says, "I quit." The head of the monastery replies, "Good! You've done nothing but complain since you got here."

Blamers and Whingers are the reverse of the monk. They can summon up a complaint on a fine day with a tail wind behind them and good fortune by their side. It doesn't matter how good things are; things will never be good enough for them.

Great Blamers and Whingers of history:

- Lady Bracknell
- Catherine of Aragon.

How to spot Blamers and Whingers

This group contains the whiners, the moaners, the grumps, the cantankerous, and the perpetual complainers – and that's the most pleasant of them. For these people, complaining isn't just a hobby; it is a reason for existing.

A day without offloading a few problems is a day wasted. A pain not shared is a pain wasted. They will be the first on the phone with the bad news.

Have you ever noticed that the people with the most complaints are also those who are often least willing to do anything to fix those complaints? It's almost as if there is a set quota for complaints that doesn't vary according to circumstances. Rain, hail or shine, the number of complaints remains the same. Once we realise this, we have a way of understanding Blamers and Whingers.

Diagnostic checklist for Blamers and Whingers
- Complain about others
- Are frustrated with the lack of wisdom in others
- Point the finger
- Are guilt-traders
- Take it personally
- Can give it but can't take it
- Know how to hold a grudge
- Have poor-me syndrome
- Are relentless in complaining (their most active aspect)
- Love to share the bad news around
- Conceal a fear of being responsible.

These tricky people can make you feel guilty and resentful. You are never quite right, whatever you do.

Favourite phrases
- "I don't want to be a bother, but …"
- "You know I'd do it myself if I could …"
- "It's all right for you …"
- "It's not my fault!"

The goal of their behaviour

Superficially, Blamers and Whingers are trying to offload responsibility. They can't accept themselves. They strengthen their egos by amplifying others' errors.

Key strategies

- Blaming others for events that are beyond anyone's control, such as traffic jams, downpours, and supermarket queues.
- Being unwilling to do anything to improve a situation or their own life.
- Demanding that accommodations be made and that "special rules" be applied to them.
- Living in the past, not in the present.

In the workplace

Blamers and Whingers abound in most workplaces. They huddle together and share grievances about how it is all so unfair. According to them, every organisation is run by a group of demented imbeciles, and every innovation is met with scepticism and cynicism. They may say things like, "We tried that last year. It didn't work then and it's not going to work now."

If you are working with them, be careful: Blamers and Whingers can be a seductive group. They seem to know the ropes. Their world-weary air can seem like the seasoned wisdom of a survivor to the new worker. Their complaints seem plausible. Initially they seduce by appearing frustrated with the inability of the organisation to take on their ideas for improvement and change. If you sit with them for long enough – and I don't advise you to do so – you will discover they take no action whatsoever to create positive changes.

These back-row idea assassins can suck the energy out of even the best and brightest innovations. Joining this band of malcontents is a short pathway to a bleak and mediocre career.

If you are managing or leading Blamers and Whingers, heaven have pity upon you. To misquote P. G. Wodehouse, even in the best circumstances they may not be entirely disgruntled, but they won't be entirely gruntled either. This is not the group to try to please. Indeed, if you attempt to do so, you may place your own career in peril. Your main energies will be diverted away from your important tasks towards people-pleasing.

How to utilise Blamers and Whingers

Shrewd leaders can use Blamers and Whingers as their own early-warning system. Blamers and Whingers are the canaries in the coalmine of life. They will be the first to tell you what is wrong with an idea, and what the most negative people will find fault with. Hearing their complaints doesn't mean you have to solve their issues, but it can inform you about likely problems. Wise managers may use this to anticipate concerns and to plan for them.

Blamers and Whingers coagulate in moments of leisure and wear the sour look of people who discover someone has piddled in their drinks. Keep them busy and keep them apart. Lessen their ability to make complaints. This can be accomplished by requiring anyone who raises a problem at a meeting to present a solution at the next scheduled meeting.

You will never entirely silence their snipings and groanings. In extreme circumstances, you may need to take them aside and let them know that, while you acknowledge their disagreement with your decision, you are their manager and you expect that publicly they will be supportive of the organisation's direction. Bluntly put, they are either on the bus or off it.

If the Blamer or Whinger is your boss, heaven have even more pity upon you. The risk of this despot making you personally responsible for any setback is high. Grab your hard hat and run for cover. If you can, change positions because, sure as eggs, one day the blame is going to be directed at you.

If you can't change jobs, practise the art of strategic invisibility. One of the commonest mistakes of employees with bosses who are Blamers and Whingers is that they take it personally – they feel at fault. So ducking and weaving and being hard to find can be useful strategies. Strategic invisibility requires you to read your boss like a weather chart and to then run for dry land.

Document things carefully. Keep copies of emails and agreements. Request written directions about work to be undertaken. If there is a change of priorities over major tasks, ask for a confirming written message.

> Robert Flynn sued the electricity board for the loss of his deceased parrot. He had placed the bird in the freezer, but during a power cut she decomposed. Flynn won the case and received compensation.

In your personal and social life

Blamers and Whingers are a real delight in families and social circles too! Their "poor fella me" attitude that blames others for the life they lead can grate. "Don't blame me, I'm just having one of those lives …" could be their motto.

There are various ways Blamers and Whingers can torture their family and friends. The first is to live in the past, hold a grudge, dwell on the wrongs and never, ever, ever let others forget them. The second way only amplifies the first when the Blamer and Whinger takes a life position in which they are the only person anything bad has ever happened to – not only in their own family or social circle, but perhaps in the history of humankind.

Put these two together, add a dash of negativity, constantly dredge up and rehash past slights and misfortunes, and most family members' and friends' eyes will be as glazed as a piece of pottery.

Now for the pièce de résistance, the crème de la crème …

Whenever anyone suggests even the slightest improvement, Blamers and Whingers absolve themselves of any possibility that it could occur. In short, they practise the art of being a cantankerous grump. Some hearty old chestnuts include:

- "I'm too old to change."
- "If only I had my health."
- "It's easy enough to talk about but …"
- "I might have been able to once but …"
- "It was different when I was your age …" (it wasn't really).

While Blamers and Whingers can wield their craft at any age, it is in old age that some can really perfect it. These miserable moaners cling to life ferociously. Spending prolonged periods with them is like having a near-death experience. It's not enough to for them to continue to live; they need to make others miserable. Some of them seem to enjoy ill health and incapacity, and inflict maximum pain upon their families. Their favourite opening line is, "I don't want to be a bother, but ..."

Blamers and Whingers and romance

Romantically, these lovers trade in martyrdom and guilt. They are often the nitpickers and fault-finders of love. Blamers and Whingers have a talent for turning relationships into prisons and their partners into prison warders. They tell you they have had such a dreadful time that you become their personal carer, valet, nurse and counsellor rolled into one.

These stunted characters can't attain a full life, and need someone to blame for it – you. Minor domestic arrangements can become a major opportunity for complaint. Popular issues include:

- Toothpaste not squeezed from the bottom of the tube
- Toilet-seat cover not put down (or left up)
- Toilet roll facing the wrong way
- Who put out the rubbish bin last.

Run, my friends, run as far as you can.

If you want to have a relationship rather than a job as a prison warder or a personal carer, you will need to tread very carefully. You may need to feign deafness and develop a steely gaze that brooks no boarders.

Relationship advice from a Blamer and Whinger

1. Be pathetic, dependent and needy – never do anything for yourself that your partner can do for you.
2. If romance is not about finding the right person but being the right person, then the most important person in a relationship is you. Be as self-centred as possible. Talk about yourself endlessly. Ask your partner very few questions. If you do ask a question, don't listen to the answer.

3. Criticise, bicker, be petty, and pick faults. Expect that this will be helpful and appreciated. Give your partner "constructive criticism" in front of their friends.
4. Be boring and domesticated and dress down on all occasions.
5. Be belligerent and bossy, and insist that your way is best.
6. Don't wash – your natural juices and scents are entrancing and should be shared.
7. Never apologise, never explain.
8. Consider compliments as unnecessary.
9. Check up on him or her with the beady eye of a surveillance specialist.
10. Provide plenty of attention, appreciation and compliments to your partner's friends while supplying none to him or her directly. And sharing your opinion that these friends are "really hot" always helps.

Tricky conversations with Blamers and Whingers

- **R** Respond with respect
- **E** Engage
- **S** Seek understanding
- **O** Observe feelings
- **L** Lower the tone
- **V** Value-add
- **E** Empower

R Respond with respect

Almost every family and organisation has a "designated sufferer". This person carries the disappointments and burdens of life and wants to share these with others without ever giving any of them away. You can watch relatives at family gatherings huddle together at the opposite end of the table in the hope that they can be spared. They are the black holes into which positive ideas are dragged, never to be heard of again.

Vice-like grips on the faults of life are hard to shift. Even if you point out that the chance of being trampled by a herd of rampant wildebeests is so negligible as to be not worth worrying about, remember they only have to be proven right once to have their doubts and fears confirmed.

Blamers and Whingers are the possessors of privilege. Their pessimism often conceals the fact that they personally benefit from things being the way they are. Never expect them to admit this.

Before you contemplate responding, look in the mirror. Who among us has not been a bit of a Blamer and Whinger at some time? Have you ever fallen into the trap of blaming and whinging about a Blamer and Whinger? We can all be part of the problem at times.

Ask yourself the following:

- How have you handled complaints in your life? Who were you trying to please?
- How have you dealt with letting down or disappointing others? (We've all done our share of this one!)
- Did you rush around trying to please, salve, bandage up? Did it work? Do you think you are a people-pleaser? Do you try to please people who really aren't important to you?
- Do you get a thrill from being seen by others as a Mr or Ms Fix-it?
- Have you sometimes become an amateur social worker? Have you been secretly delighted that others need you to provide solutions? Some people have the knack of surrounding themselves with the ailing and wailing. If this is what you want, that's fine. Just don't complain about it later.

The other response to complaints is perfectionism, where you try to do no wrong. Some people who grow up in the presence of a Blamer and Whinger narrow their lives to the point where they don't attempt anything that they are not assured will be successful, in order to avoid blame.

The question to ask yourself is: "Do I really need to respond at all?" Your answer will be determined by the personal and possible toxic potential of their complaints.

🅔 Engage

Your tentative question of "How are you?" will unleash a litany of woes and miseries. Breezily shifting the conversation in a positive direction – "Isn't it great that … ?" – is never going to work.

Take a deep breath. It is best to deal with the matter directly: "I hear you have a problem with … can you tell me about it?"

Allow the complaint or issue to land. Instead of leaping to counteract inaccuracies or misperceptions, listen silently and carefully. Let their issues land. You might even rub your chin thoughtfully and say, "This is serious. I need to give this some thought before replying to you."

Unless there is some imperative for immediate action, take your time to consider what is worth acting on and what is a waste of time. Trying to remedy the issue too quickly might be perceived as being frivolous or uncaring and could worsen the situation. Thank them for bringing the matter to your attention.

Of course, it may not be you who initiates the tricky conversation. A Blamer and Whinger may bail you up unexpectedly and confront you with a series of wrongdoings and accusations. In this situation your best response is SGS:

Sorry – I'm sorry that happened to you.
Glad – I'm really glad you let me know.
Sure – I'll be sure to look into it before getting back to you.

🅢 Seek understanding

The power of complaints is felt when people try to solve them. No one likes complaints being made. Not all complaints are fair, and certainly not all complaints are solvable. Even so, some people act as if a complaint is an immediate call to action – it must be solved straightaway.

Instead, when someone complains to you, it is worth asking him or her: "Are you just wanting me to know about it or are you wanting me to do something about it?"

Too many people rush around trying to solve problems that really don't need solving. When people complain, it could be a request for a solution, but it could also be a cry for attention or understanding or just to be heard. Figuring out why a Blamer and Whinger complains will help you deal with him effectively. Nevertheless, Blamers and Whingers can use you as a human Complaints Desk.

It is different if the complaint is about something you have done or if it damages your reputation. See the action steps for Back-stabbers (at the end of Chapter 3) if this is the case.

If you are a bit of a people-pleaser (which is no crime), the longer you let the complaint about you linger, the worse you will feel. Avoiding the complainant won't make you feel better. It is best to get it sorted as soon as possible.

O Observe feelings

In the best of all possible worlds, no one would have any complaints about anything, ever. However, as Theodore Rubin once wisely observed, "The problem is not that there are problems. The problem is expecting otherwise and thinking that having a problem is a problem."

People are going to have complaints about you from time to time. Some of these will be justified; others will be outrageously unfair. Some we should try to fix; others we should try to ignore.

Be honest with yourself first. If you've made a mistake, fess up, make amends, or fix it, and move on. If the complaint is not justified, either ignore it or stomp on it. (See "Dealing with mistakes", page 55).

Developing trust in yourself, your intentions, and your abilities is the key to not letting put-downs affect you. The best outcome would be for them to slide off you like a penguin off an ice shelf. Practise unconditional self-acceptance and live according to your values.

If the complaint is unjustified and is spreading, you are going to need to stomp on it. The outcome you want here is to have the tricky person not blame, whinge, or exaggerate about you. For that you need a clear head and a steady hand.

Blamers and Whingers make complaints because it bolsters their egos. Often they are afraid of their own incompetence. They find it much easier to blame someone else if things go wrong than actually try to find a remedy.

In the film *The Life of Brian*, the leader of the People's Front of Judea asks, "What have the Romans ever done for us?" The replies mention roads, hospitals, welfare and security. The leader then says, "OK, but except for roads, hospitals, welfare and security, what have the Romans ever done for us?"

If Blamers and Whingers want to spend time finding faults in others, they have an impoverished existence. And why complain, anyway? Problems are opportunities in drag.

Remember, whenever you act without thinking, you give up your power to choose.

Lower the tone

Stomping on a complaint involves several steps:

1. Remember, not all complaints are personal attacks on you. Some are reflections of a desire for acknowledgement, attention, recognition or understanding. If you think this might be the case, try providing these things first, and see if the complaints cease.
2. If the complaints about you continue, write them all down.
3. Check that your list is accurate.
4. Ask to talk to the person. Call them aside and have a quiet word. Begin by asking them to sit down, and then ask: "What do you mean by … [whatever was said]?" If they deny it, say: "You may not be aware, but others are telling me you've had some complaints about things I have done. These are the complaints I've heard about …"
5. Confront the issue calmly. Maintain good eye contact and be serious. Let them know that for you to have a good relationship with them, you need to sort this out.
6. Try to be helpful without taking sole responsibility for the issue. If there does seem to be a problem worth solving, you could ask: "What would need to happen for your complaint to be solved?"

Value-add

1. Confront – ask them: "What do you mean by … ?"
2. Let them know that you have a problem with what has been said, and then ask: "Do you have a solution you can suggest?"
3. Warn the person nicely that you will not put up with such behaviour in the future.

4. Be prepared to confront whenever you need to.
5. You may wish to publicly correct misinformation.
6. Treat it like you are correcting an inaccuracy – you are doing them a favour.

Be assertive and calm and conciliatory, but also make it clear that you won't accept that behaviour. And once you have confronted the Blamer and Whinger, and they have changed their ways, offer friendship and cooperation.

Empower

One of the likely reasons you have been vulnerable to Blamers and Whingers is that you want people to think well of you. Inadvertently this has led you to try to respond to and solve the complaints of others. Mostly this has worked, but it has also caused you to sometimes allow other people to say negative things about you that are unfair.

Blamers and Whingers can teach us a few valuable lessons, including realising that:

- Nobody, including you, is perfect.
- What other people think of you is none of your business.
- You are not the only person this has happened to – i.e., don't personalise.
- Life gets very boring if you always look for others' faults.
- Being petty wastes valuable time.
- You need to confront inaccuracies a.s.a.p.

They can also teach us how to practise unconditional self-acceptance, and how to own what is ours (the accurate part) and be clear-sighted about what is not.

Blamers and Whingers

Dealing with mistakes

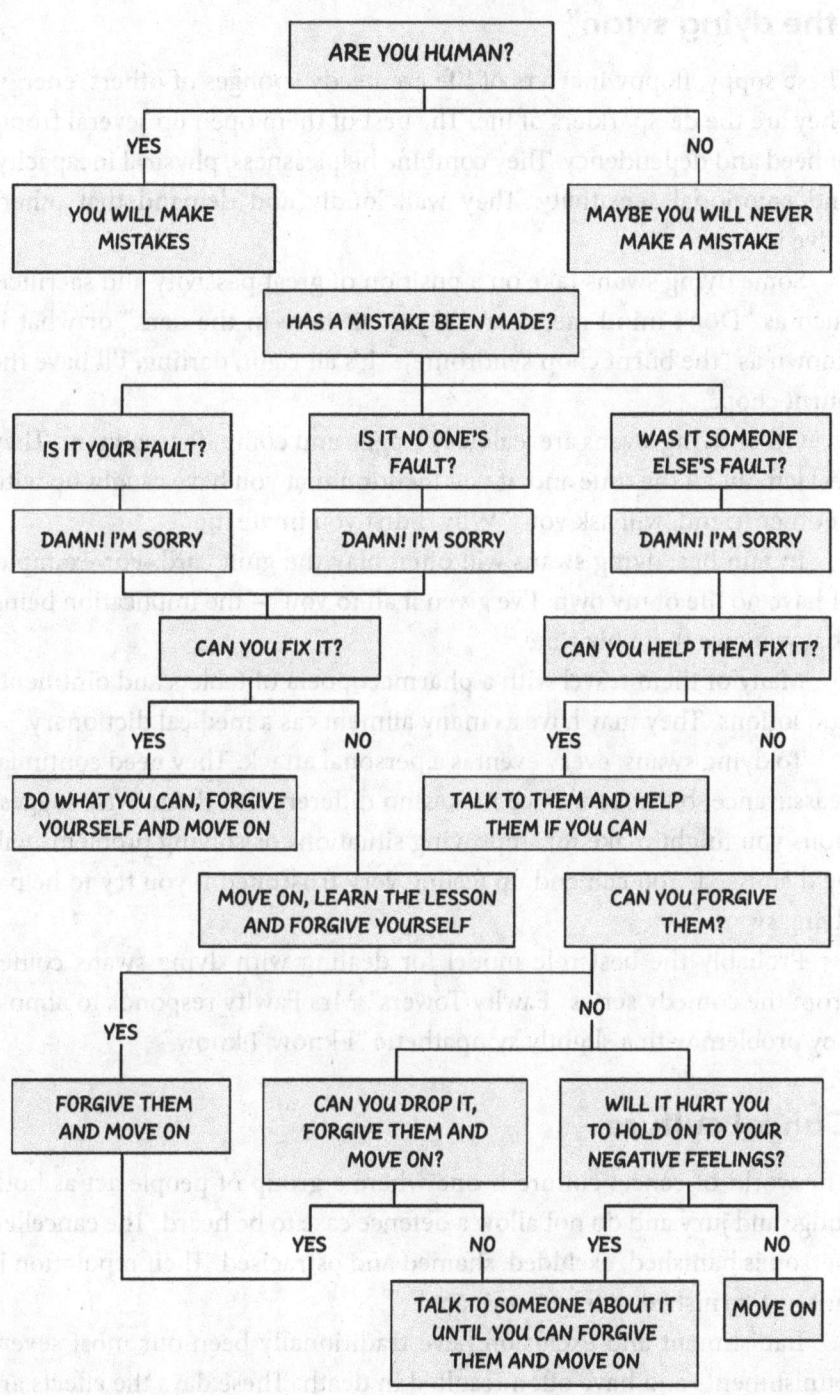

A special type of Blamer and Whinger: "the dying swan"

These soppy, floppy martyrs of life are needy sponges of others' energy. They are the de-sparklers of life. The best of them open up several fronts of need and dependency. They combine helplessness, physical incapacity, and emotional sensitivity. They wail loudly and demand that others solve it.

Some dying swans take on a position of great passivity and sacrifice, such as "Don't mind me, dear, I'll just sit here in the dark" or what is known as "the burnt chop syndrome": "It's all right, darling, I'll have the burnt chop."

Other dying swans are jealously fragile and compare treatment. They feel left out all the time and, if you mention that you have caught up with another friend, will ask you: "Why didn't you invite me?"

In families, dying swans will often play the guilt card. For example: "I have no life of my own; I've given it all to you" – the implication being that you owe them big time.

Many of them travel with a pharmacopoeia of tablets and ointments and lotions. They may have as many ailments as a medical dictionary.

To dying swans, every event is a personal attack. They need continual reassurance, but reassurance makes no difference to them. Any suggestions you might make for improving situations or solving problems will be dismissed. You can end up feeling very frustrated if you try to help a dying swan.

Probably the best role model for dealing with dying swans comes from the comedy series "Fawlty Towers". Mrs Fawlty responds to almost any problem with a slightly sympathetic "I know, I know."

Cancel culture

The world of cancel culture is one where a group of people act as both judge and jury and do not allow a defence case to be heard. The cancelled person is banished, excluded, shamed and ostracised. Their reputation is not just tarnished; it is exterminated.

Banishment and exclusion have traditionally been our most severe punishments and have often resulted in death. These days the effects are no less damaging. I have seen in my therapy room many young people who have attempted to end their lives after being cancelled from a friendship group.

The cancelling group become a vigilante mob filled with moral righteousness and what they regard as justifiable hatred and disdain. This can lead to strict conformity, harsh cruelty, and an unwillingness to forgive.

The sense of bleak shame and deprivation experienced by someone who has been cancelled has been well described by Haruki Murakami in his novel *Colorless Tsukuru Tazaki and His Years of Pilgrimage*.

Even if the cancelling group move on, the deep shame and alienation remain in the mind of the cancelled person. This is a shockingly damaging act with no redemption and no chance to plead for an alternative explanation of events. The silent treatment is often given to the cancelled person.

The cancelled person is faced with two tasks. The first involves self-forgiveness and re-establishing a sense of dignity. For some this takes time.

The second task is to rebuild a life with new networks and meaning. The establishment of a new reputation will be a vital part of this.

Action steps: Blamers and Whingers

What do they want?	How should I respond?
No responsibility	The fastest way to defuse a Blamer and Whinger is to thank them profusely for everything they do to help your family, yourself, or your organisation
Attention	"Tell me more so I can really understand this; I've got that it is important"
Acknowledgement	"I can see things have been tough for you"
Understanding	"It must seem to you that you are the only one ..."
Recognition	"I appreciate that you have worked hard to ..."

Chapter 5
Bullies and Tyrants

"Tragedy is when I cut my finger. Comedy is when you walk into an open sewer and die."

Mel Brooks

Bullies and Tyrants are merciless cowards who will take any opportunity to build themselves up and lord it over others. Some become cock-a-hoop and glide around gloating over their own magnificence and importance. Others are snide, malicious sneaks who use innuendo, rumour and tattle-tales to bring others down. Either way, they are tricky people to be wary of. These parasites and life-sappers will take your energy and self-belief away from you.

This group includes the power-hungry, the bossy, the stand-over merchants, the sly, the malicious and the dictators, all of whom have had a serious empathy by-pass. Bullies and Tyrants are insatiable. Feed their gluttony for glory, and they will come back to dine on your shattered self. The power that they gain at your expense is intoxicating – they will find cunning and ruthless ways of getting more and more of it from you.

Bullies and Tyrants are like sharks circling, ready to pounce at the merest sign of fear. And it is when you don't even know that you are swimming with sharks that the danger is the greatest. Once you can identify them as sharks, you have some choices and control.

Everyone will have the misfortune of meeting at least one of these fledgling psychopaths in their lifetime, so let's spend some time identifying them and working out how to cut off their supply lines.

Great Bullies and Tyrants of history

- Adolf Hitler
- Winston Churchill
- Idi Amin
- Pol Pot
- Nicolae Ceausescu
- Ivan the Terrible.

How to spot Bullies and Tyrants

The most common forms of attack used by Bullies and Tyrants are:

- Verbal abuse
- Stand-over tactics
- Rumour-mongering
- Gang tackling.

Bullies and Tyrants usually have a preferred modus operandi. Very likely, they developed it when they were in school, found that it worked for them, and so kept doing it.

Verbal abuse is direct; it can be nasty but it can be dealt with. Demeaning or inappropriate comments about sexuality and appearance, dismissive or hurtful remarks about your opinions, ethnic background, religion – you name it – these vipers will use anything about you to clutch at power.

Bullies and tyrants often use a few stock phrases or labels to demean others. Learning these and working out ways to topple them is worthwhile. Some possible responses are listed later in this chapter.

Diagnostic checklist for Bullies and Tyrants

- Abusive
- Demanding
- Threatening

- Insulting
- Humiliating
- Purposeful
- Dismissive of others' needs
- Inconsiderate
- Belittling
- Make unnecessary personal attacks
- Conceal feelings of jealousy
- Give you "death glares"
- Try to gain power at your expense.

> Jimmy Watson ran a legendary wine bar in Melbourne that continues today under the guidance of his son, Alan. A tourist who had drunk a few too many was carrying on about how dull and boring Melbourne is. "Melbourne," he exclaimed, "is the arsehole of the earth." Jimmy paused for a moment, looked at the tourist, and enquired, "Just passing through then, sport?"

Some Bullies and Tyrants use their physical presence to intimidate others. Stand-over tactics can include literally looming over you, staring, intruding into your personal space, and holding entire conversations with parts of your body other than your face. Find a way to move further from the bully. One woman whose co-worker would use his physical bulk to block her and to obscure his salacious gestures from other colleagues would announce loudly, "Please move, I'm about to throw up."

Some Bullies and Tyrants are talented at recruiting henchmen or henchwomen who will do their dirty work for them. These mindless sidekicks may gang-tackle you, circulate rumours about you, isolate you, and demean you. Partly because they gain courage in groups, Bullies and Tyrants are often powerful presences who attract weak followers, who then mimic their behaviours.

> *"First they ignore you, then they laugh at you,*
> *then they fight you, then you win."*
> Mahatma Gandhi

Favourite phrases
- "I am entitled."
- "You ... [add insult]!"
- "Loser!"

The goal of their behaviour

The twin goals of bullying are to dominate others and to avoid domination.

Key strategies

- They usually possess only a limited range of strategies.
- More often than not, they will inadvertently signal their next move, which might help you to identify their favourite patterns. (More on this later in the chapter.)

> "Friends may come and go, but enemies accumulate."
> Thomas Jones

In the workplace

Unfortunately, workplaces can be fertile feeding grounds for Bullies and Tyrants. Dominance hierarchies abound, and a small whiff of power goes a long way. A common piece of wisdom in one office was, "Give Bruce a little bit of control and he becomes uncontrollable." Welcome to the brutal law of the jungle.

More people leave their workplaces because of mistreatment and bullying than for any other reason. It can be incredibly traumatic. Unless that trauma is dealt with, it can infiltrate into your life.

In many workplaces, there is a pecking order that determines who is "in", who is "out", and who gets to push whom around.

Look carefully around most workplaces and you will see the primal world of territory and dominance. Who is prancing around in an alpha-type way? Who is primping and preening and trying to gain membership to the "in club"? Who is lurking in their cubicle, licking their wounds after the latest humiliation? It really is rather sad and puerile, isn't it?

> "It is a great thing for leaders that most men do not think."
> Adolf Hitler

Bosses who bully can create toxic workplaces, where people work longer hours than they should, feel anxious about taking leave that is owed to them, worry about recording devices in meeting rooms, and feel fretful if they have to take a toilet break.

If your manager is a Bully or Tyrant, the situation is very sticky. Even so, just silently enduring bullying costs you dearly. You will have heightened levels of stress, probably lose sleep, get grumpier, and increase your risk of serious illness. You could raise the issue like this: "I know you want our team to be productive and successful. I find that if people [insert relevant behaviour: "yell at me", "stand over me", etc.], my productivity actually decreases." In extreme circumstances, you may just need to refuse to put up with the shabby behaviour of Bullies and Tyrants. Record bullying behaviours and incidents, as you may have to notify higher management or your union.

If you are working with Bullies and Tyrants, you may find they will use any leverage to gain a purchase on your life. In some organisations, where you sit in the staffroom or which coffee mug you are "allowed" to use determines your position in the pecking order.

If you are managing or leading Bullies and Tyrants, you will need to lessen the opportunities for jostling and sniping. Any organisation or team contains a hotch-potch of people with varying needs. Some will be looking for a friendship group or potential lovers, and others for a replacement family, while others still are actually there to work. You are running an organisation, not a nursery or a welfare agency. Be tough-minded about your team. Be prepared to lead.

Being a leader with clear expectations of respectful and professional interactions at all times between staff members reduces bullying in the workplace. Be prepared to be proactive and to spell out your expectations with great clarity, and be ready to back this up with swift action if they are contravened.

In some professions and trades, taunting and playing tricks on new employees has become part of a toxic bullying culture. This make-fun-of-the-new-guy/gal culture has resulted in serious injuries and substantial court settlements. If you are managing a team, eradicate this culture.

Know your staff, and have great job and role clarity. Know who works well as part of a team and who uses team situations as self-aggrandisement, then allocate tasks accordingly.

If you are in charge, be in charge. Bullying, grandstanding, and malicious behaviour escalate when the lines of accountability are not clear. Jostling for position is maximised when leaders in organisations abrogate their responsibilities, become fearful or indecisive, or defer to populist appeals rather than making the tough decisions they ought to make.

As a leader, there are several ways of lessening the chance of bullying in a workplace:

- Be in charge.
- Create clear and high expectations of professional behaviour.
- Be fair – don't play favourites.
- Develop systems and routines that place customer or client care at the very basis of decision-making.
- Be clear in all communications.
- Focus on outcomes, and let staff work out the best way to achieve these.
- Be proactive about raising potential acts of bullying with the people concerned, and make it clear they won't be tolerated.

Making Bullies and Tyrants work for you

If someone is bullying others, let them know their interactions are unprofessional and need to change. Pronto! Bullies and Tyrants rarely like their behaviour to be described as what it is.

Some workplaces become so infiltrated by bullying that it almost appears normal to the workers. I once consulted to a "team" whose members behaved towards each other in horrendous ways. They would back-bite, name-call, and spread rumours, as well as sighing or yawning loudly when certain employees made suggestions. I felt as if I had just been transported out of the adult world of work into a rather vicious, rule-less primary school playground. Actually, primary school children generally act more maturely than this mob did. Eventually I said to them, "You may be used to treating one another this rudely and badly, and you may all be prepared to put up with it. I am not prepared to put up with it. Call me when you are ready to work professionally." They were aghast.

Of course, Bullies and Tyrants may also have their uses for managers. Many a successful leader has had a second-in-command with the social conscience of a Rottweiler on a diet. Using them as henchmen and henchwomen to take on tough matters is a possibility, but you'll need to have a plan to move them on before you get it in the neck.

There is a wonderful story told by author Armistead Maupin about a group of Bullies and Tyrants who boarded a cable car in San Francisco and demanded that the homosexuals identify themselves so they could beat them up. There was silence from the passengers until one brave person piped up, "I'm queer." Then another added, "Me too." Others then joined in – "I am as well" – until every passenger was claiming to be queer. The bullies, overwhelmed by numbers, retreated.

There is power in calling bullying out for what it is and gathering support wherever you can.

In your personal and social life

Being bullied by belligerent family members or friends is no fun at all. In fact it's poisonous for you.

One of the most common forms of family bullying is sibling rivalry. This generally happens when your sister or brother decides you are more loved than they are. This provides them with a reason to put you down, and to thereby increase their own esteem. With aggrieved siblings, it is best to agree with everything they say, tell them they are wonderful, and then go on being true to yourself. Sadly, times of grief can accentuate bullying and divisions. If inheritances are perceived as unequal – kaboom!

Typically in a social setting, bullies use humour to demean people:

- "She's always been a bit uptight."
- "He has long pockets and short arms."
- "If she had a brain cell, it would be lonely."

Using humour, in turn, to deflect is powerful, and often perplexes the Bully or Tyrant – something along the lines of "Oh, and I always thought you were a kind person."

Bullies and Tyrants and romance

Love and romance with a Bully or Tyrant is a perilous journey. Of course no one starts out as a Bully or Tyrant in a romantic relationship. In the heady days of seduction, all is charming and passionate. Then, subtly, the balance shifts. She starts to gently persuade you that to do things her way is better. If you fail to see the wisdom of approaching things her way, the degree of coercion increases, and before long she will be bludgeoning you into doing things her way (also see Chapter 6 on Controllers and Gaslighters).

In romantic relationships, you deserve better. Being harangued and bullied or tyrannised is horrible. A partner that does this on an ongoing basis is not a partner. She is not a soul mate, she is a cell mate, and a relationship with her will end up feeling like a prison. If you are feeling unsure, go and ask trusted friends or family members whether they think you should stay in this relationship. Even if you decide to ignore their advice, keep talking to them about the relationship.

Romantically, we can recall Glenn Close in the film *Fatal Attraction*, when, spurned by her married lover, she boils his child's pet bunny.

The short answer is: don't stay with people who bully you! The reality is: this is often not as easy as it sounds.

Tricky conversations with Bullies and Tyrants

- **R** Respond with respect
- **E** Engage
- **S** Seek understanding
- **O** Observe feelings
- **L** Lower the tone
- **V** Value-add
- **E** Empower

(R) Respond with respect

Being bullied is awful. It can rattle and plague you. Its effects can reach far and wide into other areas of your life, so it is important that you do not put up with any bullying or tyrannical acts by others.

Being bullied can be such an upsetting experience that it can be hard to think clearly about what to do. So, responding to Bullies and Tyrants needs careful planning. Don't rush in. Plan carefully and gain some allies to help you think through your options.

There are two patterns to look for in yourself. The first is a historical one. What have you traditionally done when people have bullied you? Have you felt victimised and put up with it? Avoided them? Fought back? Critically analyse your history.

Write down the strategies that have worked, as well as those that haven't. A strategy is successful if it leads to a reduction in bullying, whether you think you did anything active to cause this or not. If you can't think of a single instance where you have successfully changed a Bully or Tyrant's actions, don't worry – this chapter will help you devise a cunningly successful plan.

The second pattern to examine is your current movements and responses. Draw a map of the area where you encounter the Bully or Tyrant. This might be your home, school, workplace or neighbourhood. Note down, for a week, every time you meet the Bully or Tyrant. Write down where you meet and the time you meet. You may also like to jot down what they said or did that felt to you like bullying.

During this week, don't respond to the bullying; just observe. The less you say, the better. This is the basis of advanced surveillance of your Bully or Tyrant. Knowing where they go, when they go there, and what they do places you in a more powerful position. You need to go "behind enemy lines". Bullies and Tyrants are not very self-aware people, so being able to anticipate their actions increases your power.

 Engage

We'd love all Bullies and Tyrants to become enlightened souls who give up their terrorising behaviour, repent, and sincerely apologise for their hurtful ways. Bullies may not do this, but they can change their behaviour. Hopefully, fixing your relationship with them will help them learn that there are better ways to be with people than tyrannising them.

At work, it can be complex. Adult workplace Bullies and Tyrants rarely change their ways. While resigning from your job and moving on can be an option, economically it may not be in your best interests.

Notice what the hierarchy does to protect people who are bullied. Some organisations actively intervene to create non-bullying cultures, but others leave victims out for the wolves. The behaviour of people in meetings and the degree of professional courtesy in listening to a range of opinions may be a guide.

Investigate external forms of support in this situation, such as mediation, counselling and support from family members or senior management.

Even if you have the power, never forget that some organisations actively punish people who stand up for their rights. They treat these people as whistle-blowers and ostracise them.

Complete the analysis of your power base (see Chapter 2). Are you powerful enough? Should you confront, deflect or run for the hills?

 Seek understanding

A complete intolerance for being disrespected is the best outcome. This will require you to reduce your level of anxiety and to insist on being treated with respect.

In places of employment, this means creating an environment where everyone can express themselves and work effectively.

In a family, this may be the establishment of a clear pecking order based on consensual rules.

In love, the issue is more clear-cut. If a friend or a romantic partner continues to bully you after you have told them how you feel, your best option is to end the relationship. This might sound obvious, but many people who feel bullied by their partners never actually say to them, "When you do [x], I feel hurt, and I'd like to ask you not to do that." Ask them to stop. If you ask them to stop and they don't, it's time to leave. Sometimes you have to be prepared to burn bridges – some things are just inappropriate.

You can take some wind out of their sails by simply saying, "Let me see if I understand your position. You are concerned that ..." Sometimes they may cool off just by hearing what you understand from their side. This also helps to buy time.

 Observe feelings

Most people get bullied at some stage in their lives. It leaves them with emotional scars. These scars generally don't appear on the skin; they appear as the scent of fear, and it is this scent that Bullies and Tyrants pick up on and direct their barbs at.

The scent of fear is fuelled by a paralysis of action. You don't know what to do, so you do nothing. Analysing the situation and selecting the best course of action will help you feel more confident and smell less of fear, even if you don't take action.

One woman had a colleague who muttered "Bitch" under her breath every time she passed by. So, the woman decided to say to herself, "That's Ms Bitch to you." Even though she never said this out loud, the bullying stopped.

 Lower the tone

Bullies and Tyrants rely on predictable responses from their targets. They are used to using force to get their own way, and are used to having others quail and give in. The art of selecting strategies is to throw the Bully or Tyrant off their usual game.

Your body language is really important. When you are around Bullies or Tyrants, stand straight (don't hunch or flinch), and walk slowly and steadily. If they wish to fling an insult at you, don't feel obliged to stop and respond; sometimes it's best to keep moving and pretend you didn't hear.

When encountering a Bully or Tyrant, it is best to briefly make eye contact. Furtively looking away and hoping they will pass by generally invites an approach. Keep your head up, hold your body open and symmetrical, and keep your voice calm and low (not rapid or trembling).

Some of the strategies we use in crisis teams are useful to apply in these situations.

Positioning is important. In any tricky conversation, the top priority is always to keep yourself safe. If you are talking to a Bully or Tyrant, do so either on the move or somewhere where you can move away. Don't allow yourself to get cornered. For example, in a workplace, if approached by someone who has bullied you previously, stand up and move away from your desk and closer to the door.

Stand about one and a half arms' length away from the person. Stand at an angle with your right foot closest to the person and your left side furthest away. While I don't wish to be overly dramatic, I don't wish you to receive a punch to your heart. Practise this in many conversations, so you don't really need to think about your positioning in a potentially threatening situation.

People often signal their next move firstly with their feet. Observe where their feet are pointed, as this will often indicate to you where they are likely to move first.

The other signal that is useful to watch out for is an increase in pacifying or self-soothing actions. We all have these and use them when we feel agitated. They include:

- Rubbing nose, especially the bridge of the nose
- Rubbing lower arms
- Rubbing behind ears
- Yawning
- Playing with hair
- Head scratching.

If you see a sudden increase in these behaviours, be wary and ensure that you position yourself with your safety in mind. You may also want to lower your volume and slow your rate of speech.

Don't allow someone to stand over you while you are sitting. Don't allow someone to block a doorway or exit point. If they try to do this, say: "Excuse me, but I need to get through there." If they refuse to move, say: "I don't want to shout out for help; please move now." If they still won't move, start shouting.

Developing a thick skin and a firmness in your convictions is probably the best defence. Keep yourself safe.

Words like "concerns" and "interests" can reframe a conflict as a problem two people need to address together: "I'm concerned about …", "You seem concerned that …", or "I am interested in hearing …"

And if a Bully or Tyrant says something offensive, such as a sexist or racist remark, you can reply with something like: "You know, I never took you for a racist/sexist person. I'm surprised!"

Another approach that can be effective is using uncomfortable silences. When someone launches into a tirade, sit there quietly and thoughtfully throughout, as well as when it is finished. There is no law that says you have to have a response to everything at any given moment. Just listening might actually give you more power in the interaction, but you have to do it consciously and deliberately.

If the Bully or Tyrant is ranting, wait until they have to take a breath and then say: "If you continue to be verbally abusive, this conversation/phone call is over, and we'll continue when you have better control of yourself." Then wait for a response. If the person gets it together, continue. If not, either hang up or get up and leave. Don't allow yourself to get railroaded into making a response in anger. Follow the 24-hour rule: if a Bully or Tyrant is ranting at you, calmly say: "I need a day to think about this" and then leave. It is far better than responding in anger.

Insist on being treated respectfully and take the high road away from the situation.

 Value-add

Bullies and Tyrants are usually quite limited people who will struggle to have good friendships in their lives unless they change their ways. Many of them have learned that this is the only way they can have power. Some of them even confuse compliance with friendship. Bullies and Tyrants usually do not feel good about themselves in some way. Unless they change their ways, they often end up feeling lonely.

This, of course, doesn't mean you need to put up with them. In fact, seeing them as hostile, stunted, nasty, mean and obnoxious characters can give you a bit of distance from their toxic behaviour. One person I worked with would wait until the Bully or Tyrant was out of earshot and then say to himself, "Damned fool doesn't know any better." Another would tell herself, "What do you expect from a pig but a grunt?"

If a Bully or Tyrant has been pushing your life around for a while, change can feel scary.

There are several gradual steps to this:

1. **Know your enemy.** Drawing a map (discussed earlier) helps with this. Also keep a record of the times and types of bullying. Give yourself time to observe them – be a spy. As mentioned earlier, Bullies and Tyrants are not very reflective people so, after a short period, you will often know more about them than they do about themselves.
2. **Act like someone else for a while.** Think of someone you know of (maybe a TV or film character, a friend, or a sportsperson) who would be more able to stand up to the tyrannical behaviour. Don't intervene with the Bully or Tyrant yet; just act like this person around them. This changes the impression you are giving. In fact, you may feel like jelly on the inside while acting like steel on the outside.
3. **Learn "the Art of Invisibility".** Use your knowledge of the Bully or Tyrant's movements to generally be where they are not. Drop out of sight and go to ground.
4. **Develop security shields.** Decide which of the Bully or Tyrant's behaviours are intolerable and should be changed, and which are neutral and can be ignored. Develop a few words or responses, and practise these in your head when the Bully or Tyrant is around. This will help you to smell less of fear.
5. **Think about trying some deflection methods.** Find someone you trust away from the situation to practise these on.
6. **Always remember that you can ask higher authorities to intervene on your behalf.**

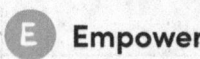 **Empower**

One of the reasons you may have been vulnerable to Bullies and Tyrants is that you care about the opinions of others. Inadvertently this has led you to tolerate behaviours you probably shouldn't have. It has also caused you to feel fear and anxiety.

Bullies can teach us:
- How to be assertive when the bullying starts
- Not to let bullying behaviours escalate
- To seek help early
- How to retain self-respect in the face of criticism
- How to face up to our fears and have clear boundaries
- How to expand our own boundaries.

The art of humorous deflection

Humour is the most powerful way of disempowering a Bully or Tyrant. Don't retaliate; deflect. Never confuse retaliation with effective action against Bullies and Tyrants. Thoughtless aggression can make you look bad-mannered and ridiculous to others, and may well worsen the problem.

The best deflecting comments disempower the Bully or Tyrant's words or use humour to change their meaning. Some examples are listed below.

The responses you make do not always have to make sense. In fact, Bullies and Tyrants are often thrown by a quick "Thank you so much for thinking of me" or "I refuse to have a battle with someone who is unarmed".

Some bullying terms and responses

The all-purpose, fits-all-situations reply to a Bully or Tyrant who is accusing you of personal deficits is to sigh deeply and say: "Yes my partner [or most of my relatives or friends] would agree with you most of the time. How can I help you?"

Bullying term	Literal definition	Possible response
"Arsehole"	As stated	"Your interest in my bottom is a bit worrying"
"Bastard"	Illegitimate child	"No, my parents were married" or "Have you met my parents?"

Bullying term	Literal definition	Possible response
"Bitch"	Female dog	"Your interest in dogs is also a bit worrying" or "That's Mrs Bitch to you!"
"Dickhead"	Penis brain	"Thank you, I could use another one"
"Fool" or "idiot".	You are of inadequate intelligence	"My IQ test doesn't show this" or "It's taken me many years to get this good"
"You have put on weight"	You're bigger	Usually something obscure, such as "It's all the sex I'm having"
"Loser"	I am better than you	"It's so good to meet a winner"
"Slut"	A person of untidy domestic habits	"How do you know I haven't done the dishes?"
"You are so pathetic"	You need help	"Thank you!"

MEMORABLE INSULTS

"Behind every great man, there is a surprised woman."

Maryon Pearson

"He is simply a shiver looking for a spine to run up."

Paul Keating

*"I feel so miserable without you;
it's almost like having you here."*

Stephen Bishop

Chapter 6
Controllers and Gaslighters

"I have never hated a man enough to give his diamonds back."
Zsa Zsa Gabor

Great Controllers of history

- Hadrian
- Catherine the Great
- Margaret Thatcher
- Joseph Stalin
- Mao Zedong
- Torquemada (Spanish inquisitor).

A mother of two grown men turned curtly to her two daughters-in-law and instructed them to get out of the range of the camera, as she wanted a "family photo" to be taken.

A boss looked up from his desk and took in his most recent employee – me. "Son," he drawled, "there are two types of bosses in the world. The first are nice, sweet people who you forget as soon as you leave them. Then there are absolute pains who you never, ever forget. And son, I want you to know in advance, you are never going to forget me."

That boss wasn't alone. According to legend, former Queensland police minister Russ Hinze was caught speeding on a country road by one of "his own" police officers. After he asked the officer, "Do you know who I am?", the officer still insisted on doing everything by the book.

Russ then heaved his considerable bulk out of his car and spread a map of outback Queensland on the bonnet. He sighed, looked at the police officer and said, "Well, son, which distant part of this fine state would you like me to post you to work in?"

Welcome to the world of tricky conversations with Controllers and Gaslighters!

How to spot a Controller

This group contains the control freaks, the pedants, the outcome-obsessed meddlers, the end-justifies-the-means operators, the micro-managers, and the nitpickers – and that's the most broad-minded of them. Controllers are people who are happy if things are going their way. Veer away from their wishes, however, and you will see an entirely different side of them.

Controllers are living proof that absolute power corrupts absolutely. They can railroad you in directions you don't want to go. The worst of this group are zealots who know they have the solution to every problem, the right course of action for any dilemma, and the correct answer for you.

When there is only one right way to do things, all that leaves is a lot of wrong ways. For Controllers there is only one way to live life – theirs.

> *George Abbott (1562–1633), when he was vice chancellor of Oxford University, sent 140 undergraduates to prison for failing to remove their hats in his presence.*

> "When I am right, I get angry. Churchill gets angry when he's wrong. So we were often angry at each other."
>
> Charles de Gaulle

Diagnostic checklist for Controllers
- Don't like surprises (and not that keen on spontaneity, ingenuity, flexibility or creativity)
- Are rigid, inflexible and unbending
- Are unable to see things from anyone's perspective but their own
- Are clear about directions but unable to take on others' suggestions
- View suggestions and input as threats to be squashed

- Are pushy and loud
- Control the flow of information
- May be threatened by younger work colleagues
- May be threatened by lively, happy family members
- Are dogmatic and dictatorial
- Conceal feelings of insecurity and anxiety.

Favourite phrases

- "This is who I am; deal with it."
- "There is only one way to do things around here: my way."

Controllers use an exhaustive and relentless array of strategies and phrases to achieve their desires. An example of tricky conversational control is outlined below.

Where have you been?
> *I was just running a few errands.*

Well, I expected you here earlier.
> *I'm sorry I was late. Are you OK?*

I'm fine.
> *You don't seem fine. In fact, you seem a bit upset.*

Don't worry about it.
> *Is there something I can do to make everything OK?*

I shouldn't have to tell you. You should know.
> *What should I know?*

If you really loved me, you would know how to make me happy.

The goal of their behaviour

- To avoid anxiety by having everything planned and predictable
- Power, or at least the illusion of it.

Key strategies

- Making ultimatums
- Placing restrictive prohibitions on others, such as, "If you do that ..."
- Some Controllers can sabotage and deviate to get their own way. For example, they may sabotage through gifts (e.g., chocolate when you are dieting) or by saying "Let's laze about all day" when you are starting an exercise program.

In the workplace

If you are working with them, Controllers can take charge of you by showing you the ropes and helping you out – and before you know it, you are doing things exactly the way they want them to happen, and that course of action seems to make sense. Controllers are extremely good at making their methods look plausible, efficient and effective.

These people are experts. Got a question? Well, they will have an answer for you. Whether it is the correct answer or not. Whether you ask them or not.

Some people are happy to be controlled. It generally works out OK for them when someone else does the thinking for them. Controllers are generally benevolent to those they control.

Others have a niggling feeling that they have relinquished their freedom and autonomy.

If you are working with a Controller and feeling like this, it is time for a stock-take of what you do and why you do it in the way that you do.

If you are managing or leading Controllers, they can be powerful allies, but spiteful, dreadful enemies. Controllers often like to mark territory. Their empire does not always have to be large but it has to be inviolably theirs. In the workplaces of most Controllers you will find an orderly display that indicates the space belongs to them, often containing photos of the people or pets they control. Trophies and territories abound. Just make sure it doesn't end up being your head that is mounted on their wall.

"I would have made a good Pope."

Richard M. Nixon

Managing Controllers requires being clear about the outcomes you want and then getting out of the way. Being in the cheer squad on the sidelines is far better than being the seer who wants to steer. Stipulate the outcomes you are looking for, then let the Controller get on with achieving them.

Controllers can set up great systems for you. They often make terrific office managers and marvellous deputies. Just don't tread on their territory. Trust them with a wary eye.

And don't be surprised if they have a hidden agenda. Controllers always have a hidden agenda.

If the Controller is your manager, they will use a range of methods to exert influence, from quite subtle coaxing to blunt cajoling. Some controlling bosses are promoted beyond the level of their competence. This can send their anxiety sky-rocketing and promote a tendency to micro-manage.

Working for Controllers is like juggling live hand grenades. Their demands, as well as their mechanisms for checking up on what you are doing at all times, border on the obsessive. Find ways to keep them informed. If you become secretive, their anxiety will cause them to become wary and interfering.

In the years of economic rationalism, there was a theory of management that suited Controllers down to the ground. It was known as "the brick in the chook house" theory, and it suggested that managers should keep their staff on their toes at all times. This is accomplished by heaving a brick (a demand or an emergency) into the office ("chook house"). When this happens, feathers fly. When the feathers begin to settle again, it is time for the next brick.

Controlling through mayhem creates the sense that, while everyone else is anxious and inadequate, sitting at the centre of the cyclone, as calm as you like, is the Controller.

The apparent clarity of vision that Controllers exude is sadly very alluring to selection panels.

Some controlling managers combine their exactitude with being overbearing. They have probably read a management book or two that suggests that delegation and consultation are good practices, so they go through the rigmarole of asking for people's opinions before blithely disregarding them. Or they delegate roles and responsibilities but then can't keep their fingers out of the pie. They meddle, check up, and suggest helpful ways of achieving the outcome. They can't leave it alone. Of course, if you have a controlling boss and a controlling employee together, you can expect fireworks and possibly tears before bedtime.

Other controlling bosses are miserly with information. Some may even deliberately tell people different things or issue two similar directives (two bricks), and watch as their staff work themselves into a frenzy.

Some controlling managers equate compromise with losing. They are unable to give ground; they dig in their heels and don't budge. And even if the battle is to their disadvantage, they can do this. Be wary: controlling bosses have a long memory and a vindictive streak that they are prepared to act on.

"I'd like to thank everyone except ..."

The drinks had been poured on Friday night. After years of hard work the project was complete. The head of the department reached the podium and began his thank-you speech. He effusively thanked the whole team, even the painters, plumbers and gardeners. The only problem was: he pointedly did not thank the man who created and completed the project.

Judge your power carefully

I'll never forget a workshop I was running on the use of "I" statements. "I" statements involve making a clear statement about your own thoughts, perceptions or feelings, starting with "I". The senior management group was seated around a boardroom table. Each member of the group was encouraged to make an "I" statement. After a few banal comments like "I feel frustrated when workloads get too much", one foolhardy staff member looked his manager square in the eye and said, "I perceive that you are a dickhead." The controlling boss returned his gaze and replied, "I perceive you will be working in our country office from Monday morning." The country office was several hours from the staff member's home.

The tricky manager: know-it-all and a total bozo

It's interesting how a working relationship can resemble the dance of a new romantic union. For the first year, both parties work in concert with each other, supporting the movements, dreams and aspirations of the other. They are seen together at functions, the manager and his/her right-hand man or woman.

As the well-intended partnership enters the second year of work, things start to fall out of kilter. The boss no longer turns to his support person, fearing that the support person is gaining the upper hand. Could it be that the authority of the boss is being undermined? Suspicion grows as the one who was second-in-charge is shown to be a favourite among the staff.

The board invites the second-in-charge to join the leadership team – now the situation spirals out of control because the manager is losing power. Everything becomes a threat, to the extent that the manager insists that all matters are to be referred to him for approval.

One needs to question how a relationship can turn so bad. Why is it that jealousy and ego can dominate the lives of adults to the extent that they can sabotage a healthy working relationship? Among these sorts of people, irrational thought turns to belief and then to bizarre behaviour. The employees are drilled to the nth degree about every detail of every event that happened in the day. It is worse than the KGB! The result: everyone loses the desire to do anything. The manager takes the credit for all achievements and all ideas – no credit or support is given to the staff. It is a total "ME" show, destined for disaster.

The office Lothario

The office Lothario is a plague for many people. Dealing with unwanted sexual or romantic approaches can be a bit tiring.

There are bosses who expect all their staff to be infatuated with them and their charms. Successful men can be at risk of believing themselves to be a living Adonis, despite a receding hairline and a broadening waist.

The process of entanglement can be very subtle: "Would you mind staying behind? I have a few things I want to ask you. Can you stay late? I'd like to get your ideas about a few things? Let's chat about it over drinks. Well, it's getting late, would you like something to eat?"

If you find yourself getting mixed signals, trust your instincts and ask trusted friends how they would handle it.

Then initiate a talk with your boss before he has delivered a clear pick-up line. Say something like: "I'm feeling a bit uncomfortable around you. I've noticed you've asked me to work late alone with you on several occasions, and I want you to know that I am in a happy relationship [or 'value our professional relationship']. I would not want to give you any inappropriate signals. I hope I am clear about this because I value our working relationship."

In your personal and social life

Controllers often have the sharp eye of an eagle, the tracking scent of a beagle, and the empathy of a hyena. Not much passes them by.

If they invite you to dinner at 7:30 and you arrive at 7:33, they will exclaim archly, "And what time do you call this?"

In families, these intrusive meddlers put their noses into things that are none of their business. Under the guise of caring concern, they seduce information out of you in order to take charge.

Some play the role of medical emergency officers. After looking probingly at you and asking something like "You look tired – are you getting enough rest?", in a trice they can have your feet up on the sofa, with a cold compress over your eyes, while they search for some tablet that did wonders for their last "patient".

Others play the seniority card on family occasions. The role of Grand Matriarch or Imperial Pater can be so powerful that other family members whisper in awed tones, "You know she always has the serviettes on the left …"

Many people experience their parents as controlling. Indeed, it may be this very perception that impels the process of growth, maturity and independence.

After the war of independence that accompanies adolescence in many families is over, a peaceful resolution is the best outcome. Parents need to learn that their child has grown up, and move from a model of protective controlling to one of minimal influence. The dilemma facing parents is well put in the Zen koan (or teaching tale) that asks people to "hold on tight with an open palm". Young adults need to dampen the fierce fires of battle and accept their parents' well-intended influence without feeling directed by them.

Friendships with Controllers can be very valuable, so long as you see the clarity of their vision, wisdom and advice. Controllers love to dispense advice. Often it is far better to respond to suggestions with "That's a great idea" than to steadfastly insist on your own direction. Then quietly go off and do exactly what you want.

Controllers can be jealous of your other friends and how often you see them, so it is often best to remain quiet about the times and outings you have with others.

Some Controllers treat friendship as a combination of trespass and possession: no part of your life is allowed to be private. They will interrogate friends about the most private and personal matters. It takes a strong will to hold your ground and not reveal all.

Some Controllers are in perpetual adolescence. They can pout, sneer and throw a hissy fit like the best teenagers. They react to dissension and individuality in their friends like the most possessive adolescent, and they often sulk when they don't get their own way.

Controllers and romance

> *"If you can't live without me, why aren't you dead already?"*
> Cynthia Heimel

Romantically, Controllers are an interesting mix. Loving, caring, helpful and meticulous problem-solvers, they can be an absolute boon to your life. But hand over too much control to them and you may find basic freedoms slipping away. Controllers may want to know where you are when you are not with them. They can have surveillance methods that would impress many spy agencies. But you are not obliged to answer every prying question – it is all right to say to Controllers "That's private." In extreme circumstances, they can create romantic relationships that resemble a kidnapping: they play the part of captor while the other becomes captive.

> Dr W. G. Grace, pioneering English cricketer, was an intense Controller. Clean-bowled by Australian fast bowler Frederick Spofforth, he replaced the bails and remarked that there was a particularly strong wind for that time of the year. "Carry on, Spofforth," he commanded.

Tricky conversations with Controllers

- **R** Respond with respect
- **E** Engage
- **S** Seek understanding
- **O** Observe feelings
- **L** Lower the tone
- **V** Value-add
- **E** Empower

R Respond with respect

Controllers are very focused people. Generally, they know what they want, and heaven pity anyone who gets between them and their goals.

No one really likes feeling controlled, so Controllers cleverly start with offers of help that gradually, over time, twist into a mechanism that controls the way you act in the world.

Here are some questions to check if you have a Controller in your life. Does someone else:

- Control your diary or appointment book?
- Take charge of your social calendar?
- Choose your clothes for you?
- Control your finances?
- Administer medication for you?
- Reply to your emails on your behalf?
- Tell you what you can or cannot eat?
- Organise where you go on holidays?

If the answer to any of the above is "yes", your personal choices are evaporating before your very eyes.

Of course, having this helpful person in your life can be very useful. Do you have the energy or resources to resist the changes the Controller wants? Do you have the resources to do more things for yourself? Controllers do not want to relinquish their power. They will wrestle and dominate you and use wily ways to beat you into submission.

What eventually is at risk here is your ability to be a fully functioning person who can stand on your own two feet, think for yourself, and make independent decisions about your life.

 Engage

Engaging with Controllers (and as we'll see later, with Gaslighters) may not involve a conversation at all. It may involve awareness and action on your own part.

One of the questions to ask yourself when dealing with a Controller is: "Am I giving away my own power?"

As you'll recall, from your analysis in Chapter 2, Warriors are gung-ho, let's-get-on-with-it types; Visionaries are creative but don't like details; Healers like people getting on and dislike disagreement; and Wise Ones are knowledgeable but can get bogged down in details.

Warriors may charge off in other directions to avoid being controlled. The only problem is that, by doing the reverse of what the Controller wants, who has the power? Right: the Controller.

Visionaries usually resist Controllers with the most vengeance. They will feel stifled, checked up on, and hemmed in. Rather than dealing with the Controller directly, however, they may be tempted to avoid and evade.

Healers may submit, and often don't want to make waves. Politeness and an unwillingness to cause a scene make Healers easy targets for Controllers.

Wise Ones become cautious and guarded.

Whichever type you are, don't be a martyr. Help your organisation, but not at a cost to yourself; assist and care for your family, but not at the expense of your own well-being.

A passive acceptance of having things done around you may lead to resentment. It may be convenient, but your personal freedoms are being eroded. Not only do you become a doormat in the process, your Controller's demands will usually only escalate.

Feeling imprisoned or interrogated by a Controller may lead you to take on sneaky behaviours to escape him.

Think about occasions in your life when you had power but did not use it. There can be many reasons for deferring to Controllers: it can be easy, you may feel it is polite, you don't want to make a fuss, you feel it is all too difficult, you don't want to hurt their feelings, and so on. It can be easy to develop dependent behaviour when the Controller has solved all your problems.

 Seek understanding

> A multimillionaire was staying at a hotel and went for breakfast. During the breakfast service a waitress distributed one bread roll to each diner. The multimillionaire looked outraged at his solitary roll and demanded another. After being told the policy was one roll per diner, he raised himself to his full height and yelled, "Do you know who I am? I am the richest man in this city. I could buy and sell this hotel several times over. I could have you fired. I demand another roll." After a lengthy pause, the waitress replied, "I'm very pleased to meet you, and I'd like to introduce myself. I'm the lady who serves out the rolls!"

You are the person with the rolls! If you didn't have the "rolls", the Controller probably wouldn't be interested in trying to control you.

While it is tempting to think the best outcome is to have the Controller rack off and leave you to live your life, the best outcome is actually more about you than him. The preservation of your right to make your own decisions is the best outcome. Your own ability to be a fully functioning adult is at stake. Obviously you will make considerate and compassionate decisions in an egalitarian environment that is not controlled by anyone.

Independent management of problems and the ability to problem-solve for both people are the aims of any intervention.

ⓞ Observe feelings

The desire to control is a very ancient and primitive way to ward off anxiety. It occurs in most species and is the basis of pecking orders. Controllers are quite anxious people. If they gain control, they obtain a sense of predictability that then lessens their own anxiety.

Variability may threaten Controllers. The world does not act in predictable ways. It is not controllable. This means Controllers are on a pointless quest: the more they fail to gain control, the more they will seek to have control. All in all, it is exhausting work that can make them deeply unhappy. Controllers may well fall apart if they can't control relationships or environments.

Your options include:

- Thanking the Controller for his interest and following his suggestions
- Thanking the Controller for his input and ignoring his advice
- Telling the Controller to mind his own business and stop bothering you
- Avoiding the Controller until he gives up

While heading for the hills or getting sneaky can be appealing, you should deal with a Controller directly. Calmly point out that you have an alternative and independent way of doing things, and you are going to do them your way. Don't apologise and ask if that is OK with him (even if you are asking sarcastically). Don't ask for permission to act independently. Reassure the Controller that things will be fine. Demonstrate your own independent behaviour. Be less reliant on the Controller. Model that your independence does not equate to a threat to him. If you can have him gain from your independence, that is also desirable. Learn how to deal with Controllers' number-one weapon: making ultimatums.

A brief word on ultimatums: don't give in to them!

Lower the tone

Calm, independent behaviour on your part may give you freedom and may also reassure the Controller that they are not the only responsible person on board. Change the language used by Controllers for coercion and compliance to requests and voluntary agreements.

Controller says	You respond with
"I demand that you ..."	"You would like me to ..."
"I want you to ..."	"You're asking me to ..."
"I expect that you will ..."	"So, what you were hoping was ..."
"If you don't do ..."	"You'd be upset if I didn't ..."
"Don't you ever do ..."	"You'd be disappointed if I ever ..."

One technique that works with Controllers is called "shifting the world". Controllers aim to have you act in predictable ways. To loosen up a Controller, you may decide to vary your routine dramatically.

Gradually increase your spontaneity. Shift your schedule. Make erratic entrances and exits. Keep them well informed if you need to but start acting in quirky ways.

Moving from a routine to flightiness will bewilder Controllers. It may increase their controlling acts in the short term, but in the long term they will acclimatise to your wayward ways.

While being as changeable as a flea in a dog pound, remain friendly and positive. Reassure the Controller that things will be fine. This will help your Controller to learn that you may be a loose cannon, but your waywardness is no threat to him. Give this a good six weeks to take hold.

 Value-add

In all dealings you have with Controllers, assume equal and cooperative functioning and communication. Insist on solving your problems yourself; lessen your reliance on them. Don't allow them to intervene with other people on your behalf. Be consistent about this and don't let them slip back into either helping you or making decisions for you.

Reclaim your personal power. Don't allow Controllers to manage the flow of information to you. If they screen your calls, make your bookings, or set up your appointments, find some pretext for changing this arrangement.

 Empower

One of the reasons you have been vulnerable to Controllers is that you don't like to worry other people; you are polite and caring, an agreeable person. Inadvertently this has led you to going along with the demands of others. It has also caused you to sacrifice part of your own independence.

Controllers have many useful lessons to teach you. These include:

- Never give up your own independence and control of your life.
- Be aware of that hemmed-in feeling – having things done for you, although initially pleasant, comes at a cost.
- There is no such thing as a free lunch.

> A newly married couple had trouble gaining privacy from their well-intentioned but meddling and controlling parents. Neither partner had lived away from their parents prior to marriage.
>
> On the weekends, when they wanted to spend some private time together, in would pop one or other set of parents offering to mow lawns, fix guttering, bake cakes, and so on. Unsurprisingly, the couple didn't want to offend their helpful parents, so they decided on a cunning plan. The next weekend when the parents visited, the couple exclaimed, "Thank goodness you're here. Would you mind fixing the side gate? And would you be so kind as to weed the garden?" The couple then went inside and turned on the television.
>
> It wasn't long before they overheard rumblings from outside: "I think they have become too dependent on us" and "I think it's time they learned to stand on their own two feet!"

Gaslighting

Martha (not her real name) was referred to me for treatment of her kleptomania. Her partner had told her she had a personality disorder.

Martha had been charged with a series of minor incidences of theft from large department stores. Intriguingly, she could not recall ever taking the items that had been discovered in her bag by the security guards. We considered possible dissociative and fugue disorders with memory loss. After some sessions, it became apparent that on all occasions she was charged she had been shopping with her partner and had carried a large handbag with her. It eventuated that her partner had placed small items in her handbag without her knowledge.

There is a sinister corner of hell especially reserved for Gaslighters. I need to believe it. If you are afflicted by one of these malevolent vipers, you need to believe it too.

Gaslighters have a nasty technique of causing their victims to question their sanity and their reality. This can involve distorting the truth. It can also involve flinging casual diagnostic statements at someone, usually beginning with the words "You are too [insert a diagnostic label: sensitive, anxious, paranoid, protective, jealous, temperamental, needy, arrogant and the list goes on]."

Some will use a tactic of "bait and switch", where they make a humiliating comment only to retract it later with "I was just joking" and an insinuation that you are overreacting.

Social media has created a special type of Gaslighter: the conspiracy theorist. These are people who jump on any piece of information, regardless of the validity or verifiability of the source, as "proof" of their personal conspiracy theory. Anyone expressing doubts about their theory is labelled as a deluded pawn.

One way of understanding gaslighting is through Sigmund Freud's concept of projection and Carl Jung's concept of shadow, in which a person takes the parts of themselves that they cannot abide and sees them in someone else. An example of this in a tricky conversation is: "I wouldn't get so angry if you weren't so [insert a diagnostic label]."

Gaslighting can be intensified after the break-up of a relationship. The logic seems to be: "Anyone who doesn't want to be with me would have to be crazy. Therefore, my ex has to be crazy, and I will devote a lot of time to proving this to the world (even though I never want to see them again)."

Being gaslit is bewildering. It shakes your confidence and leaves you second-guessing yourself.

Always seek a second opinion from a trusted confidant. If need be, seek out a third or fourth opinion as well. You might be able to co-exist with a Gaslighter by continually stating "Let's just agree to disagree. We see things differently." However, it is highly unlikely that a Gaslighter will ever take responsibility for his or her actions (even when shown undeniable proof). They have not much ability to change.

How to be controlled by giving away your power

It is amazing how many clever and otherwise talented people give away their power. There seems to be no end to the ways people find to do this, so here we can only offer a beginner's guide to the most common ways.

1. **Convince yourself you should not have personal power.** Power is your ability to influence outcomes. It can be used positively as well as negatively. Some people don't use the power they have by convincing themselves that having power is a bad thing. If you don't have or use your power, others will.
2. **Don't take time to think about what you want.** This is the number-one reason people don't get what they would like. Most people spend more time planning their holidays than thinking about the type of life they want. If you don't think about the life you desire or the type of world you wish to live in, then any power you do have is wasted.
3. **Say "yes" when you mean "no".** It is good to be agreeable, but not being able to say "no" when you want to erodes your ability to have an influence. You will end up doing what other people want. Not making a fuss, being reasonable, and fitting in are all positives, but if you spend too much of your life's energies on what others like and not enough on what you want, you risk ending up bitter.
4. **Don't ask for things you want.** This is a peculiarly passive position in which people expect the world to magically provide for them.

Expecting others to mind-read what you desire provides great proof that telepathic communication doesn't exist.

5. **See others as better informed and as having superior knowledge, skills and intelligence.** This allows you to give away your power by assuming someone else will deal with things. There will always be people who are smarter and more capable than you. Don't wait for other people to act before doing what you know to be right.
6. **Pay more attention to what people say and less to what they do.** Actions really do speak louder than words. The most reliable predictor of what someone will do in the future is never what they say they will do, but what they have done in the past.
7. **Allow others to dictate to you.** Let others present the options to you. Avoid making decisions for yourself.
8. **Be busy and flustered.** Talk about being overwhelmed – people will believe you.
9. **Blabber about all your intentions, plans and ideas.** Sharing ideas is all well and good, but sometimes it is better to act than to become known as a "could-a-been" who talks a lot but achieves little.
10. **Isolate yourself.** Be distant and unapproachable. Don't ask for help or seek others' opinions. This will minimise the number of allies you have and lessen the positive impact you can have in the world.

But if you do want to make an impact and have an influence, try the following ideas.

How to gain power and make a positive impact on the world

1. **Know what you want.** Take time out in a frantic world to think and plan. Most people spend their lives reacting to events and to changing circumstances. Think about the outcomes you want and write them down somewhere private.
2. **Practise pathological simple-mindedness.** Once you have an idea of the impact you want to have, focus your energies on it. As most people are scattered, clearly directed energy often gives them clarity, and they can help you achieve the outcome.

3. **Have some failures and setbacks.** They teach you persistence and resilience. Powerful people do not have fewer setbacks than others; they simply don't let failure stop them.
4. **Hold your own counsel.** Use fewer words. The world does not need to know your views and thoughts on everything. Consider issues and be prepared to wait and watch rather than rushing to judge and evaluate. Events and people are not always what they seem to be.
5. **Guard and manage your reputation.** Your reputation is your most powerful ally. Your image is within your control. Be conscious of how you want to appear to others. Be prepared to confront people who malign your reputation.
6. **Be humble.** Let your actions speak for you. Be generous. Give credit where credit is due and sometimes where it is not due as well. Make others feel important – it makes them want to associate with you.
7. **Highlight similarities and conceal differences with others.** People trust people who appear to be the same as they are, and many people assume that others are like them. Look for ways to have something in common with most people who are important to you.
8. **Step off the well-trodden path.** While still highlighting similarities with others, do things your own way. Create a distinctive style that attracts attention. Be more of you. Sometimes think about what everyone else is doing and make a conscious decision not to do that. Be calm and measured. In a frantic world of rushing about and time poverty, one of the simplest ways to stand out is to be tranquil. The best way to be peaceful is to practise pathological simple-mindedness.
9. **Stand on the shoulders of giants.** Let the greats of the past and present influence you. Access big ideas. Read well and be informed.
10. **Dream big dreams.** Be prepared to dream a vision for the world you want, and then be bold.

Action steps: Controllers

What do they want?	How should I respond?
Security and reduction of anxiety	With firm unpredictability
Not to feel threatened	Reassure them you are no threat; if they rail at you, calmly say you will talk to them about this at a later time
To erode your power via ultimatums	Know that ultimatums come from a position of weakness
"Do it my way, or else!"	Don't oblige them; demands escalate if you give in or try to appease

MEMORABLE INSULTS

"He had delusions of adequacy."

Walter Kerr

"He loves nature in spite of what it did to him."

Forrest Tucker

"His mother should have thrown him away and kept the stork."

Mae West

Chapter 7
High and Mighties

"Is there no beginning to your talents?"
Interviewer Clive Anderson to author Jeffrey Archer

Great High and Mighties of history

- Duchess of Windsor
- Noel Coward
- Oscar Wilde
- Marie Antoinette
- Dame Edna Everage
- Gore Vidal.

How to spot a High and Mighty

This group contains uppity snobs, the smug, oh-so-superior people, the cads, and the whiz-bang supermen and superwomen. The higher moral ground is often claimed by absolute scoundrels.

The High and Mighties appear to have a surplus of self-esteem, and in their esteemed opinion other people aren't really worth the time of day. The great unwashed, in their view, are beneath contempt.

High and Mighties expect that others will recognise their true brilliance and superiority, and often throw temper tantrums when their special, unique magnificence is overlooked. One young woman

I encountered recently was quite well known for looking down her nose and saying, "I'm too pretty, too skinny, and too tanned to speak to you."

To misquote author P. J. O'Rourke, for High and Mighties, the main problem with the world is too much of you and too little of them.

Diagnostic checklist for High and Mighties

- Are snooty and superior
- Are smarmy but can be charming
- Are lone rangers (do not work well with others)
- Hate to compromise
- Are derisive and disapproving
- Tokens and symbols of success mean a lot to them
- Want the best office, the closest car park, the most gifted child, and the most luxurious home
- When annoyed, may ignore other people's greetings
- Can be posh snitches
- Gather supporters, acolytes and disciples
- Anxious and may have low self-esteem
- Fear they won't measure up.

Favourite phrases

- "I am so offended that you could believe …"
- "How dare you!"
- "Have you seen the latest …?"

Acronyms to describe High and Mighties include:

- FIGJAM – "F**k I'm good; just ask me."
- LOMBARD – "Lots of money but a real dickhead."

The goal of their behaviour

- Personal advantage, attainment of privilege
- To cover up fears that they may not measure up.

Key strategies

- Always claim the higher moral ground

- Assume that they are the only people with sufficient good sense and taste to be able to enlighten the drab masses
- Use helpfulness and high-handedness as guises to ward off those who do not recognise their superiority.

In the workplace

High and Mighties can be quite useful in the workplace. They often seem to gravitate towards the desk with the best view, have a penchant for the best coffee, and seem to make the most of their leave entitlements.

They often glide into work and announce that they have just been to the best restaurant, show or holiday spot. Everything they do is bigger, better, brighter, more important and certainly more stylish than anything the likes of you could dream up. Their ideas are fresher, more creative, and incredibly smarter than yours. Just between you and me, they privately wonder how a barbarian like yourself was ever selected to work in a place like this.

These gilded lilies think they are doing you a favour just by being there. If you have any type of inferiority complex at all, High and Mighties will bring it out and make it squeal. If you are working or living with them, there is an essential lesson to learn: Don't compete with them.

> *"Moral indignation is jealousy with a halo."*
> H.G. Wells

> **When the fox is away**
>
> I once had a manager who was a High and Mighty. Lauren would spend the budget and travel the world. She was very good at coercing you into doing things her way. She grandly referred to "her staff", "her management team". She outsourced work to her friends and would offer to rewrite colleagues' material – and then publish it under her own name. After my first run-in with Lauren, after she had published my work under her name, she called me regularly. She would phone me when I was with clients, asking, "Where are you? What are you doing?"

> Her fatal error was to appoint a business manager she didn't really know. Gayle was ambitious from the outset: she told anyone who would listen that she'd be the next CEO.
>
> Gayle waited till Lauren was overseas on one of her many business trips. I was called in by Gayle and her cronies to add my signature to a letter of no confidence in Lauren. I refused.
>
> At an emergency meeting of the staff with the board, Gayle laid down an ultimatum: "Either sack Lauren, or I reveal to the public how badly this organisation is mismanaged." Lauren was sacked the day she returned. My only thought was: the new High and Mighty has arrived.

In the workplace, High and Mighties love to use obscure terms and acronyms. These are used to denote who is in the know and who is not. If you have to ask what the latest jumble of letters actually means, you will receive a pitiful look and an exalted explanation. If you require clarification about what exactly Form 33.1B, subsection D is used for, your naïve and rustic ways are exposed to the world.

Sadly, High and Mighties are quite capable of using your ignorance as a source of mirth with the in-crowd behind your back. While you may well feel humiliated and seethe, relax – their time will come.

High and Mighties have a talent for turning other people's envy valves on full bore. You may find yourself wanting to prove that you too go to great restaurants, shows, plays and places. If you, through gritted teeth, make a comment to the effect that they always think their own choices are the best, they will barely bat an eyelash before announcing, "I was only trying to help."

High and Mighties control others by making them feel inferior, and then by having them play the game of catch-up. It's a clever ruse that allows them considerable sway and influence over the unwary.

Know clearly that whatever you do, wherever you go out to eat or go on holiday or buy a house, it will never, ever, ever be as good as the things that they do. And once you know how despicably, tastelessly lowbrow you truly are in their eyes, you can sit back, be amused, and start having a fine old time.

One of the great games you can play with High and Mighties is to find the most execrable, mindless television shows, plays and activities, and share these with them in a "You must go and see ..." manner. Then sit back and watch their eyes roll as they try to maintain a gracious stance while absolutely abhorring your taste. There is a lot of fun to be had in being deliciously low-brow.

As High and Mighties are awfully successful at attracting acolytes and apostles, or "cling-ons", you may want to quietly let a colleague in on the joke.

> **High and Mighties who live in glass houses ...**
>
> A High and Mighty was shopping in an expensive department store and accidentally broke a highly valuable vase. Upon being told that the vase would need to be paid for, the High and Mighty asked for it to be gift wrapped and sent to a friend who was about to have a birthday. The friend received the beautifully wrapped broken vase. In fact, the vase was so beautifully wrapped that each broken piece was wrapped separately.

If you are managing or leading High and Mighties, they can be a bit daunting at first. They clearly hold dim views about your capacity to fulfil your job. How you ever managed to be promoted over them is a mystery. They have deep suspicions about your intelligence, proclivities, judgement and lineage.

Working with High and Mighties has a couple of potential pitfalls. Generally, they don't like getting their hands dirty, so if there is muck to be raked, expect them to be handing you the gardening tools. Also, if trouble is brewing, they will be sorely tempted to make you a scapegoat.

High and Mighties won't wait for a staff appraisal to gain feedback about their performance. They will be the first to provide pats on the back. It's just that the back they will be patting is their own.

It's only when you realise that High and Mighties are addicted to being associated with exemplary things that they become easy to manage. Allocating tasks to them that "only you could do" or confiding in them that "You know how important it is that we raise standards and productivity here" are good places to begin.

If you are managing or leading High and Mighty employees, be warned that they are insatiable. Nevertheless, they love being associated with exemplary products, places and people. If you can convince them that they are privileged to work where they work, they will primp and preen. Giving them positions and projects with prestige will keep them industrious and focused.

If one is your manager, your main job – regardless of whatever job description you might hold – is to make them look good. If a High and Mighty boss loses face, someone else generally loses a job.

"The Rooster"

We had a regional manager we called "The Rooster" because he got up early and crowed about himself a lot. A couple of times a month, he blew in from afar to tell us how it was going to be. The wafts of cologne and the Armani suits should have been a give-away.

He loved to convene consultation meetings in which he would ask for ideas and input, which he then duly ignored. He gave lip service to teamwork, and his definition of compromise was that he got exactly what he wanted and "stuff the lot of you". He never did any work at all.

In your personal and social life

A High and Mighty may cast a weary eye around the table at a family gathering, survey the collected pack of misfits and assorted gorillas, and wonder how they came from such lowly stock. Alternatively, they may have a high opinion of the genetic purity of their ancestry, only to give others a look that seems to say, "How the heck did you fall out of my family tree?"

One of the great games families can play with High and Mighties is called "remote-control roulette".

Remote-control roulette

This game often emerges naturally in families with a High and Mighty member, because the tricky person swans in and, regardless of what is being watched on TV, grabs the remote, announces there's a show on (something that is clearly more intellectual, artistic and supremely worthwhile than anything you could be watching), breezily says, "You don't mind, do you?" and, without waiting for an answer, changes the channel.

Remote-control roulette follows the rule that the person who holds the remote selects the show. Now let's not forget: from the High and Mighty's perspective, if you have the remote, it is in the hands of someone who thinks that professional mud wrestling is as intellectually stimulating as a chess tournament. Sure, Shakespeare was good, but he's not one of the Kardashians. So, in those times when you want a bit of privacy, play up to those fears about your base nature. In fact, try to set a new all-time low for finding the most mindless, puerile pieces of nonsense on television. Everyone deserves a little fun now and again, especially you.

As friends, the High and Mighties can be good fun, but again only as long as you don't compete. If you go out to eat with them, don't expect to select the restaurant – they will always have a special place they know. They will confide in you that the owners are personal friends. With some of them, don't even expect to be able to order your own food. And an evening spent catching up with them can feel like a slow week at "Camp Inferiority".

One rather amusing High and Mighty friend of mine entered a wine bar with a great flourish, pranced up to the counter, and announced to the barman, "I'll have my usual, thanks". The barman, while polishing a glass, lifted one eyebrow and dryly asked, "And what might that be, dear?"

Negative High and Mighties

A woman was at the hairdresser getting her hair styled for a trip to Rome with her husband. She mentioned the trip to the hairdresser, who responded: "Rome? Why would anyone want to go there? It's crowded and dirty. You're crazy to go to Rome. So, how are you getting there?"

"We're taking Continental," was the reply. "We got a great rate!"

"Continental?" exclaimed the hairdresser. "That's a terrible airline. Their planes are old, their flight attendants are ugly, and they're always late. So, where are you staying in Rome?"

"We'll be at this exclusive little place on the Tiber River called Teste."

"Don't go any further. I know that place. Everybody thinks it's going to be something special and exclusive, but it's really a dump."

"We're going to go to see the Vatican and maybe get to see the Pope."

"That's rich," laughed the hairdresser. "You and a million other people trying to see him. He'll look the size of an ant. Boy, good luck on this lousy trip of yours. You're going to need it."

A month later, the woman again came in for a hairdo. The hairdresser asked her about her trip to Rome.

"It was wonderful," replied the woman. "Not only were we on time in one of Continental's brand new planes, but it was overbooked, and they bumped us up to first class. The food and wine were wonderful, and I had a handsome 28-year-old steward who waited on me hand and foot.

"And the hotel was great! They'd just finished a $5 million remodelling job, and now it's a jewel, the finest hotel in the city. They, too, were overbooked, so they apologised and gave us their owner's suite at no extra charge!"

"Well," muttered the hairdresser, "that's all well and good, but I know you didn't get to see the Pope."

"Actually, we were quite lucky, because as we toured the Vatican, a Swiss Guard tapped me on the shoulder and explained that the Pope likes to meet some of the visitors, and if I'd be so kind as to step into his private room and wait, the Pope would personally greet me.

"Sure enough, five minutes later, the Pope walked through the door and shook my hand! I knelt down and he spoke a few words to me."

"Oh, really! What'd he say?"

He said: "Where'd you get the shitty hairdo?"

High and Mighties and romance

Romantically, High and Mighties are on the big dipper of love. They can swoop you up with grand flourishes of love and devotion. To be worthy of the affections and desires of a High and Mighty, you must truly be pedestal material. Alas, it won't be long before you are no longer worthy of this glorious love that they have to give. Don't share your flaws or imperfections with them. Burping and slipping into the trakky dacks is not the pathway towards ongoing romance. If you want to stay in a romantic relationship with a High and Mighty, scarcity is your number-one friend, and familiarity your number-one enemy. With past loves, you may have been able to spend lots of time together. High and Mighty lovers have a lot going for them, but you need to play hard to get and harder to keep. Scarcity equals desirability. Pause for a time before returning calls. Try to only accept every second or third invitation from them.

As High and Mighties love being associated with exemplary people, places and things, you need to regard yourself as absolutely top-shelf material. Being a self-effacing shrinking violet is not going to cut it.

One of the thoughts that sabotages relationships for High and Mighties is the gnawing concern that they "could do better". They may never say this directly to you, but in the back of their mind it will be ticking away. This means trouble for those of you wanting to love High and Mighties. At the slightest hint from them that they are better than you, you need to walk away fast and only return after pleading or gifts – or, even better, both.

This is the great paradox of a successful relationship with a High and Mighty: to save it, you must risk it all by being prepared to walk away. For if you try to save it by tolerating their snooty sniping, you will surely lose it.

This means that loving a High and Mighty is not for the faint-hearted. For those of you prepared to be bold and, at times, elusive, the best awaits you: the finest restaurants, the most artful films, and some lovely holidays.

Just click your fingers – and be prepared to pout!

Tricky conversations with High and Mighties

- **R** Respond with respect
- **E** Engage
- **S** Seek understanding
- **O** Observe feelings
- **L** Lower the tone
- **V** Value-add
- **E** Empower

E Respond with respect

High and Mighties can be a hoot as long as you don't take their sneering personally.

You need to consider whether competing with and confronting them is really worthwhile; often ignoring them or enjoying them is a better strategy. How much damage can a High and Mighty cause you? They may lord it over others for a time, but it won't take long before people wise up. In some instances, responding may be necessary, but generally having a sense of humour and perspective is more useful.

> *"When the great lord passes, the wise peasant*
> *bows deeply and silently farts."*
>
> **Ethiopian proverb**

High and Mighties are very good at playing on any feelings of inadequacy or insecurity you may have. They know exactly the buttons to press, and delight in doing so.

Based on our analysis in Chapter 2, Warriors take the battle up to High and Mighties, as they don't like feeling beaten, and loathe playing second fiddle. A generally frosty relationship occurs between Warriors and High and Mighties.

Visionaries blithely disregard High and Mighties but may underestimate them and their level of influence.

Healers are often bedazzled and awestruck by High and Mighties. Healers may feel delighted to be included in their world and may play the role of an admiring audience. Healers are vulnerable to being dominated and ordered about by High and Mighties.

Wise Ones are usually watchful and wary and tend to sit back and keep a suspicious eye on these gilded lilies.

 Engage

The best outcomes with High and Mighties may have more to do with changing your own perceptions rather than their behaviour. The best outcome may be to regain your confidence in your own abilities, taste, style and choices. Despite their tendency to roll their eyes and murmur "Really!" when they see your latest acquisition, you can enjoy the access and the luxury they can provide you.

High and Mighties can take you out to the finest places, introduce you to the finest wines, and try to impress you with the best books, films and shows. Be flattered. Behind the snooty airs of a High and Mighty lies a disguised desire to gain your approval. You can't see yourself as a god if you don't have any disciples.

 Seek understanding

High and Mighties are trapped on the treadmill of having to impress others. Before you start feeling too sorry for them, they are usually too busy basking in the glow of their own magnificence to realise this.

Amusement at the behaviour of High and Mighties may seem a bit sneaky; laughing at them silently may seem a bit mean. Even so, a wry chuckle is not going to hurt anyone.

If you really want to torment a High and Mighty, counter-offer something that is even better. If they mention a fabulous show/film/book/piece of kitchenware they have seen, you might like to say, "Oh thanks. I've heard that is good, and that [another show/film/book/piece of kitchenware] is fantastic, too." This will cause a flurry on the part of the High and Mighty to demonstrate to you why their selection is better than yours. Even though they will be certain their selection is the superior one, there will remain a nagging doubt.

If you really are set on changing a High and Mighty's ways, you will need to foster cooperative behaviours, so you don't feel inferior. This may cause some turbulence before you reach the destination of "wary regard".

Generally, don't compete with High and Mighties – it will be like water off a duck's back. Make a firm decision to regard yourself well; regain the belief that you are just as worthwhile.

O Observe feelings

In your life, it is likely you will have encountered people who thought they were fantastic while you were considered to be scarcely a boil on the backside of life. Have you always fallen for this? Have you allowed yourself to be deluded by their superior airs and ways while you struggled to aspire to mediocrity? You may also have felt resentful that you needed to flatter them when you didn't want to.

Some people spend their lives trying to prove themselves to High and Mighties. They come in many forms: disapproving parents or in-laws, bosses, commanding colleagues, snitchy relations, snooty friends, and the extremely beautiful "You-can't-believe-how-lucky-you-are-to-be-with-a-jewel-like-me" romantic partners.

I have seen many people in therapy who have devoted their lives to seeking approval from people who are dead. If you are seeking the approval of a High and Mighty, always ask yourself: "What would that approval look like, and how would they indicate to me that they approve of me?"

You can end up being swept up on a mission of proving your worth, or even your right to exist, to a High and Mighty. Good luck! You'll be on a mission that will make the quest for the Holy Grail look like a stroll in the park.

Lower the tone

In many primary school playgrounds, a vicious game is played: the game of "who is in and who is out" or "who plays with whom and who is not allowed to play at all". It is the most hurtful game that children play. This game is repeated in the world of cancel culture, which resembles the banishment and ostracisation of medieval times.

One of the best ways of viewing High and Mighties is as primary school students who are stuck at that stage. They have never grown up and are still playing the game of "If you are my special best friend, you can play with me; but if you aren't, you can't."

High and Mighties are insecure. The shadow that we talked about earlier (see Chapter 1, as well as Chapter 13) looms large and lurks deep in them. They secretly believe they may not be good enough – that's why they behave in such snooty ways.

Keep in mind that they are very good at the game of "in groups" and "out groups" and at times you will lapse into trying either to prove yourself to them or impress them. You are enough, as you are.

 Value-add

Increase the sense of humour you have around the actions of High and Mighties. Become untouchable by viewing their superior ways as reflecting their own feelings of inferiority.

Deliberately role-play the opposite of a High and Mighty. Get low-down and dirty, low-brow and tasteless. Think of the tackiest TV show/piece of art/poem/song/novel and sing its praises to them. You can enjoy watching their withering appraisal of your complete lack of taste.

 Empower

One of the reasons you may have been vulnerable to High and Mighties is that you are humble. A bit of humility is a charming quality in people; a lot of it, though, can get a bit dull. There's not much point in looking at the stars if you're heading straight for the gutter. Inadvertently, your humility has led you to think that High and Mighties are brighter stars in the universe of life. It has also bewitched you into believing you are fortunate to be included in their orbit.

There is a difference between being humble and being emotionally frail. It is time to learn that you can also be strong. You deserve the best as much as anyone does.

Recognise your own feelings – only you can make yourself feel inferior. Search out self-defeating thoughts and lessen their power over you. Some common self-defeating thoughts are:

- The contentment robber – "I did that well, but I'm sure it was because [insert some external factor or piece of luck]."
- The bravery robber – "If I get this wrong, it will be a disaster. [Insert High and Mighty's name] would never get this wrong."

Make a pact to challenge yourself whenever these thoughts enter your head. It's an enlightened day for all of us when we finally realise that not every idea that enters our heads is equally wise. Some are, in fact, just plain stupid.

People who are vulnerable to High and Mighties may also apologise too often or may excuse themselves when there is nothing to excuse. Good manners are a wonderful thing, but this is a living, breathing, pitiful apology for your own life.

Give yourself a maximum number of apologies you are going to make each day and see if you can stick to it for a while.

High and Mighties have some positive lessons to teach you. Watch and listen, and you will learn. Learn, for instance, how to be a good guest – you may have fun going to a great play or being taken to the finest restaurant.

Also, High and Mighties are sponges for positive feedback, compliments and flattery.

Develop the gentle art of flattery, and have some fun with it …

> *"He is a self-made man and worships his creator."*
>
> John Bright

Action steps: High and Mighties

What do they want?	How should I respond?
Prestige and power	Demonstrate that you are comfortable in yourself
Image	Everyone has their own image; you don't need to compete
To pat themselves on the back	Their self-congratulation need not affect you

Tricky Conversations

What do they want?	How should I respond?
Reassurance that they are really OK	Reassure them that you like them for themselves, not just because of the things they do
Your approval	Provide it in bucket-loads

MEMORABLE INSULTS

"He has no enemies but is intensely disliked by his friends."

Oscar Wilde

"He has all the virtues I dislike and none of the vices I admire."

Winston Churchill

Chapter 8
Avoiders

"Santa Claus has the right idea. Visit people only once a year."
Victor Borge

Great Avoiders of history

- The Scarlet Pimpernel
- Casanova
- Ronald Biggs
- Lord Lucan
- Eva Peron.

How to spot an Avoider

This group includes the lazy, the indirect, the infuriating, the escapologists, and the sneaky culprits – all of whom suffer from an extreme form of responsibility-itis that could be called the "Who pooed in my pants?" syndrome.

Have you ever seen a three-year-old toddle up with obviously full pants and a surprised look on his face as if to say, "Who pooed in my pants?" Well, Avoiders are a lot like that.

Unable to face up to even the most obvious of their actions, they wheel and deal to get out of it. Avoiders come in various types, but they are all commitment-phobic and allergic to accountability. With subterfuge and sleight of hand they can weasel out of even the most watertight guarantee. These shirkers and timewasters can be harder to pin down than mercury.

One group of Avoiders is people who can't say what they want:

Would you like to go to a movie?

That would be OK.

What would you like to see?

I don't mind, whatever you would like.

How about ... ?

That's fine.

[Later] What did you think of the movie?

Well, it wasn't really my type of film anyway.

Others lack sequencing and organisational abilities and avoid when the task at hand overwhelms them. They may lack the ability to acquire the skills needed and, when faced with a new task, may hide and think "What the ^%$# do I do now?" These people might delegate because they don't know what to do and hope you will complete things for them. They could also be simply whimsical and dreamy, space cadet–like, rather than malicious.

Avoidance, to them, is a coping mechanism. Avoiders might be diabolical at budgeting and organising functions; the whole thing could go belly-up. Direct communication may also be a problem.

Some may be superficially charming – they have developed the art of flitting in and out with ease.

Avoiders typically have jobs that require them to be on the road a lot, leaving a trail of damage as they go, often blaming others for their own lack of organisation.

Diagnostic checklist for Avoiders

- Don't show up – when the heat is turned up, Avoiders go on leave
- Are slippery
- Actions don't always match words
- Suffer from responsibility-itis and the "Who pooed in my pants?" syndrome

- Promise the world then don't deliver
- Continually disappoint you
- Cancel meetings to discuss issues because of crises, illness or vague reasons
- Seem as changeable as a chameleon
- May be a great borrower but a poor returner
- Have a fear of accountability
- Are "forgetful"
- May mask a fear of not being capable or a fear of being successful.

It's enough to make you tear out your hair! Not only do Avoiders resolutely withhold their own wishes, they then have the temerity to complain about the choice that was made. Avoiders are so indirect, they make refracted sunlight look direct.

Whenever you hear the phrase "I don't mind – whatever you would like", alarm bells should sound in your head. Announcements should come over your own internal speaker system: "Warning! Warning! Danger! Danger! Responsibility-itis attack approaching!"

Another group of Avoiders are the scaredy-cats, who prefer to lead you on a merry dance rather than face you directly. They often find it difficult to say "no" to people, suffer from the "disease to please", and avoid conflict and disagreement.

I recently consulted with a rather well-to-do girls' school. The staff never, ever argued. Not a voice was ever raised in anger.

The school should have been a place of calm and happiness; instead, the teachers looked tired and edgy. The school principal was a classic Avoider – the only way anyone knew she was upset was when she gave them flowers. The result of this was a school awash with anxiety – avoiding discussions that needed to be had.

Favourite phrases
- "I'll try." Avoiders are great triers – they try and try and try, but never quite manage to get it done.
- "I would really like to help you, but unfortunately I do not have the man hours in my budget – so what can I do?"
- "I am too busy to [do whatever task] at the moment …"
- "[Something happened], which then caused me to [xx], so I can't …"

The goal of their behaviour

The Avoider's goal is to not be held accountable. Avoiding may be a subconscious way of avoiding failure; they may feel overwhelmed by a task. Some of them do not have the ability to acquire skills, and avoiding is a coping mechanism. Others may have issues with paying attention, which means they miss key information, and thus misunderstand tasks and/or deadlines.

Key strategies

- Smoke and mirrors
- Equivocation, evasion
- Forgetfulness
- Sudden mystery illnesses.

In the workplace

If you are working with Avoiders, try not to get into group projects with them – because guess who will be doing all the work? Avoiders are often pleasant, charming and reassuring people who are about as useless as a lamb chop at a vegan convention.

Some Avoiders play the "learnt helplessness" game in the workplace by saying "You will do this better than me" when in reality they are quite capable of doing it and may just be feeling overwhelmed at the prospect.

If you are managing or leading them, know that Avoiders are about as reliable as a dodgy car bought cheap from a second cousin's brother-in-law after it fell off the back of a truck. Avoiders can promise you the world and deliver nothing. These are people who don't do what they say they will.

Some are bald-faced liars who, if you ask whether a task is nearing completion, will reassure you with a cheery "Absolutely!" When the deadline nears, however, they duck and weave.

"We are not retreating – we are advancing in another direction."
General Douglas MacArthur

Avoiders

Pinning down Avoiders is a tricky business indeed. You can chase, but often you cannot find. Try to pin them down and you will witness a dazzling show of smoke and mirrors. When something is due, they may mysteriously become ill or have to attend the funeral of their fourth grandmother. If they do come to work, they may limp in wrapped in bandages, or have a crisis that means they have to cancel meetings.

When deadlines are missed, Avoiders often claim: "I'm doing the best I can" or "I didn't understand the task" or "It wasn't properly explained to me." Excuses, reasons, rationalisations and outright lies tumble forth.

But also understand that procrastination often conceals anxiety.

Avoiders can be used by shrewd managers and leaders as peace negotiators. These "good-time Charlies" often excel at praising others and making excuses – in fact, they have a master's degree in it! In tough times managers can send out Avoiders as emissaries to try to sway the disgruntled masses.

If your manager is an Avoider, it will be very hard to get direct feedback, direction or instruction. Some will divide and conquer staff by setting conflicting and ambiguous directions. Others may manage by whim – whatever yesterday's direction was is now countermanded by today's new idea.

Such bosses might say, "Here is a job I want you to do. I'm not too clear what needs to be done. You can work that out. I want it done yesterday, and you have no resources to do it with." Making sure that you communicate in writing or email (if you can) about this is essential. Write something like:

> *Dear Bill,*
>
> *Just want to make sure I've got it right. The top-priority job is ... This means the other task you asked me to do will need to be delayed. If you don't have time to get back to me before 11 am, I'll assume that's correct.*
>
> *Sincerely,*
>
> *Joan*

Avoider bosses can fail to manage anyone. At the first hint of conflict between people, they hit the road and can't be seen for dust. Some of them can be slimy and may sacrifice others so that they can remain in their position. They have mastered the art of invisibility. When the tough stuff happens, Avoiders get going – away!

If you are having difficulty with an Avoider as a manager, don't expect a lot of assistance. If an Avoider manager asks you to sort out a dispute between two other staff members, claim that you are massively under-qualified to do this. The reason is that if you start to make unpopular decisions in order to resolve the issue, guess whose support you are not going to see until the place is once again smelling of roses?

News flash! Working with idiots can kill you!

STOCKHOLM – Dills and drongos at work are just as hazardous to your health as cigarettes, caffeine or greasy food, an eye-opening new study has revealed. In fact, those dropkicks can kill you!

Stress is one of the top causes of heart attacks, and working with tricky people on a daily basis is one of the deadliest forms of stress, according to researchers at Sweden's Lindbergh University Medical Centre.

The author of the study, Dr Dagmar Andersson, says her team studied 500 heart-attack patients, and was puzzled to find 62 percent had relatively few of the physical risk factors commonly blamed for heart attacks.

When questioned about lifestyle habits, almost all of these low-risk patients revealed they worked with people so stupid that they can barely fathom how a paper clip works. And their heart attack came less than 12 hours after having had a major confrontation with one of these oafs.

One woman had to be rushed to the hospital after her assistant shredded important company tax documents instead of copying them. A man told us he collapsed right at his desk because the woman at the next cubicle kept asking him for correction fluid – for her computer monitor.

"You can cut back on smoking or improve your diet," Dr Andersson says, "but most people have very poor coping skills when it comes to stupidity – they feel there's nothing they can do about it, so they just internalise their frustration until they finally explode."

Having stupid co-workers can also double or triple someone's workload, she explains. "Many of our subjects feel sorry for the drooling idiots they work with, so they try to cover for them by fixing their mistakes. One poor woman spent a week rebuilding client records because a clerk put them all in the 'recycle bin' on her computer and then emptied it. She thought it meant the records would be recycled and used again."

In your personal and social life

Avoiders can start out being bright, charming, witty and fun, only to become the emotional black holes of the universe. These life bandits can suppress true feelings and squeeze the lightness out of any relationship – all while taking no responsibility for their side of the equation.

Friendship with an Avoider can be delightful. As long as you stick to light and happy topics, they will be a joy to be with. But try to pin them down or discuss deep issues and watch them run! Friendship with an Avoider often involves excusing a lot of lateness and even forgetfulness about agreed meeting times.

Try not to lend Avoiders money. They can be quite good at going out and "forgetting" their wallets or purses. They can borrow belongings and not return them. These evasive airheads are legendary for not paying rent on time, not returning the books they borrowed, not paying back the money you lent them, and not doing their share of the work.

Becoming a guarantor for an Avoider's financial loans is an act of sheer madness. Of course, lending very small amounts of money might be all right. As a wise person once commented, if you lend someone $20 and never see him or her again, you probably got a good deal.

For a friendship with an Avoider to succeed, you need to not lend them anything that you won't feel resentful about losing if they don't return or repay it.

Friendship with Avoiders is a hit-and-miss affair. When things are good, they will be very, very good, but when things go bad, you won't see them. If you have a falling out with them, don't expect them to be dropping in for a chat to sort the problem out.

Avoiders also include friends who say "We must catch up," and then are always unable to get together. Avoiders with a touch of the High and Mighty about them would "love to catch up" but are too busy saving the universe, curing cancer, and halting climate change to do so.

Avoiders are so good at creating excuses and escape routes, they begin to believe their own PR. Frankly, some of them couldn't lie straight in bed.

Avoiders and romance

Romantically, Avoiders can become as elusive as the Scarlet Pimpernel whenever the C-word is in the air: commitment.

Avoiders are the anaesthetists of love – they can stifle positive feelings. Some play "take-away" whenever things get too hot and sticky by changing the topic, removing themselves emotionally, suddenly becoming ill or tired, or demanding their own space.

In love, Avoiders are superficially good at closeness. They will seemingly drop all their friends to be with you; they will change plans to find space for you. They can make you feel wonderfully important and special. However, what they don't say is as important as what they do say – the past loves, wives/husbands and friends that are not mentioned. One Avoider I knew "forgot" to tell his new love that he had a whole family in another state. If you carefully sift through an Avoider's history, you will find a series of people who have been dropped like hot potatoes, never to be mentioned again.

In families, probably the most infuriating of the Avoiders are the chronically listless ones. These are Avoiders who can't make decisions and have a limited desire to achieve. Their get-up-and-go has got up and gone, and you can feel at times like checking to see if they still have a pulse. Trying to rev up and motivate listless Avoiders can be a pointless, infuriating enterprise.

One of the common patterns that parents of Avoiders get into is asking questions they already know the answer to, such as:

- "Have you brushed your teeth?"
Rather than: *It's time to brush your teeth.*

- "Have you got any homework?"
  Rather than: *It's time to do your homework.*
- "Did you remember the job interview?"
  Rather than: *I'll phone you to make sure you get to the job interview.*
- "Did you have to work late?"
  Rather than: *I know you weren't at work, so what delayed you?*

Living with an Avoider means having to be as blunt and direct as a force-ten gale.

The fine art of avoiding responsibility

Here's how to make others face up to it while getting off scot-free:

1. Claim it was never your intention to …
2. You weren't there at the time.
3. You have no recollection of …
4. The other person must have misunderstood.
5. Fess up and then claim the higher moral ground – e.g., "I did it, but I had to because …"
6. It was the previous person's responsibility.
7. "Given what I have to work with …"
8. "After all I've done, I'm trapped in a web."
9. "I can't do it alone …"

Tricky conversations with Avoiders

- **R** Respond with respect
- **E** Engage
- **S** Seek understanding
- **O** Observe feelings
- **L** Lower the tone
- **V** Value-add
- **E** Empower

R Respond with respect

You don't get many opportunities to respond to avoiders, so plan your approach carefully.

Avoiders are slippery. They can be harder to pin down than the end of a rainbow. When you have to ping an Avoider, know that you may only get one chance. If you don't get it sorted out in one sitting, they may become so elusive that you could chase them forever. To sort matters out with an Avoider, you will have to pursue, and you will have to cajole. And timing is everything. If you decide to confront them, make sure they have nowhere to run and nowhere to hide.

Hostility will not be effective; directness will be.

E Engage

An encounter with an avoider always involves a subtle, polite battle of wills. You are most likely seeking clarity and commitment, while they are trying to be flighty and evasive.

The first step is to return to the agreements. For example: "My clear recollection is that the project was due to be completed by last Friday." Be positive. Convey an air and an expectation that you can work this out.

If it is a matter of mutual understanding, raise the issue directly. For example: "My understanding was that we were in a monogamous relationship; is that your understanding?" or "My understanding was that good friends back one another and follow through on their promises; what's your view of good friendship?" or "My understanding was that the money you borrowed from me would be repaid by now; what is your understanding?"

Reduce their audience. Ideally meet with avoiders one on one. However, if you have concerns about information from the meeting being shared inaccurately later, ask an independent observer to silently sit in. It is not advisable to allow the avoider to bring a friend, support person, or other ally. The more people that are involved in the meeting, the more charm will be on display, and the more evasion you will have to deal with.

Sit them down and gain eye contact.

Define the task or issue before they flit off.

Clarify your expectations of the relationship. For example: "For us to work effectively together, I need to be sure that you will do what you say you will do. Is that possible for you?"

Expect excuses, rationales and explanations of extraordinary circumstances. Be kind but do not be swayed.

Ask them to go through procedures. If there is a job description, policy or relevant piece of legislation that is related to the matter, ask them to read it out to you. Most likely it will be the first time they have read this. Up until now they have managed to wing it.

Define the clear outcome or action you are seeking. Your aim is not their confession of evasiveness. Your aim is that they act with integrity in relation to you by being true to their word. Whatever you regard to be clear evidence of this will need to expressed to them.

If you can, do some pre-testing of this plan for possible loopholes and potential misunderstandings. It will need to be pretty water-tight to be avoider-proof.

Agree to stay in conversation until an adequate outcome is achieved.

Agree when to meet again to review progress.

Know in every cell of your body – every fibre of your being – that they will do anything and everything to avoid the next meeting. Pets will be in peril, relatives may be at risk of sudden demise, onsets of mysterious illnesses may occur. Be kind. Re-schedule if need be. You are not going anywhere.

Follow up.

Always aim for a win/win outcome with Avoiders – they can be great fun and lovely allies so long as you don't rely on them too much.

It can be useful to say to an Avoider: "X, you are a terrific person, and it has been hard to sit down and sort out a few issues. I believe you have been avoiding me. Let me tell you how it seems to me. You have missed/cancelled our last two planned meetings. You haven't kept me informed. This reflects badly on you."

Show them you know what's going on; a one-to-one discussion in private is best for this. Write down strategies and outcomes. Document agreements.

In business settings I teach leaders to say: "At the end of the day, if we can't resolve this, one of us is irrelevant, and I think you should know in advance that person is not me."

Warnings:

1. Avoiders are very good at deflecting and obscuring. As you try to get to some clarity, they will often soothingly murmur, "Do what you think, whichever way you want." They appear laid-back and superficially supportive. Lurking behind their affable manner, however, is a devious intent to find a glimpse of a fraction of a smidgen of a possibility not to be held accountable. Hold your ground.
2. If you succeed in a task, it is as they expected. If you fail, they blame you.

S Seek understanding

Resist the temptation to fall for their superficial charm. You can give them a bottom line in an equally charming manner.

Resist the tendency to compensate for their lack of planning – you may wish to be helpful, but don't sacrifice yourself in order to help an Avoider.

They are just as adult as you are. Despite their protestations, they are fully-grown people with the capacity to solve problems. They don't need another mother or father, so stop your parenting response. Let them face consequences, and make sure they take the blame rather than you.

You won't always know where you stand with Avoiders. They survive in a murky world of excuses, stories and rationalisations, some of which may even be true. You may get a sneaking suspicion that you are being taken for a ride. Trust your gut instincts: if you wait until you are sure, you may wait forever.

O Observe feelings

Avoiders would like you to fall in with their dance. As they are charming, you may feel bad about giving them a bottom line. They may make up incredible reasons why they can't come into the office, repay the loan, or return your precious items.

You may compensate for their disorganisation. In extreme cases, you may find yourself thinking ahead for them, excusing them, and not letting them face the consequences of their actions. You might even pseudo-parent them – don't: this lets them off the hook of being responsible while they get to play at being the beleaguered sook.

 Lower the tone

You may begin to feel cheated, used or abused by an Avoider. This can be infuriating, especially if you've been left waiting forever at that meeting place for that much-promised work outcome or for that repayment.

Remember that some Avoiders do this as a coping strategy because they are not up to the task. It may be useful to see some of them as more incapable than malicious. Reframe their avoidance techniques as a severe case of responsibility-itis.

Accept that you are not responsible for their inaction. Whether they are capable or not, they are responsible for their behaviour. You don't need to excuse them or let them off the hook. Do not inadvertently accept the blame for their avoidance strategies.

 Value-add

When we increase integrity in our relationships, everyone benefits. Avoiders probably won't see it, but their actions cost them dearly. People generally look for other people they can rely on and often stay away from people who let them down.

Integrity increases peace in the world because it builds trust and reliability.

1. Be very clear about what you will or will not do.
2. Keep a record of your actions.
3. Don't exhaust yourself compensating for Avoiders – you will only resent it.
4. Realise that avoidance can be a coping strategy for them.

 Empower

One of the reasons you may have been vulnerable to Avoiders is that you want good outcomes for the people in your life. Inadvertently this has led you to take responsibility for actions that are not yours. It has also caused you to excuse others for their failure to follow through.

Long term, this can encourage incompetent, sooky behaviour and responsibility-itis in others. You may have wondered why the people around you have always let you down or have been incapable of achieving agreed outcomes, when all along you were unknowingly encouraging this. It is time to let others be strong, stand on their own two feet, and take responsibility for what they do.

Key lessons from Avoiders

- Remain vigilant.
- Don't get sucked in by superficial charm.
- Sit down and discuss what needs to be done at the first sign of avoidance.
- Don't take on responsibility for anybody else.
- They are adults, so you do not need to parent them.

Are workaholics Avoiders?

Workaholics are not such a problem in the workplace unless you feel compelled to keep up with them. They are generally very able and use their vast array of talents to be very focused at work. These people appear so dedicated to their job that they do not leave till midnight, only to start again at 7 am. They may be doing this to avoid other aspects of their life, such as their family or a relationship. When these areas of life become difficult, these Avoiders retreat into the world of work. Others begin with a great creative engagement in work that contributes, through their absence, to difficulties in other areas of their lives.

Either way, they are so engaged in the importance of work that they don't have time for anything or anyone else. Some of these people may be so busy that they hold down more than one job, or they may run their own business while completing further studies. They might make you feel inadequate because you cannot keep up with such a human dynamo.

The message they give is: "Don't take it personally, but I must be off." They flit in and out of social and family relationships.

Their competence is a coping mechanism that allows them to deny their unhappiness in other areas. It is certainly not designed to make you feel incompetent.

With these people, resist the temptation to compete or feel inadequate. They are doing this to avoid areas of life that you are happy and comfortable in. If they choose to work inordinate hours or engage in Herculean tasks, that is their business. Let them! It has nothing to do with you.

Action steps: Avoiders

What do they want?	How should I respond?
To cover up feelings of low self-esteem	Give them tasks they are capable of achieving
To disguise their own incompetence	Skill development
To disguise poor sequential and planning skills	Plan and sequence tasks for them. Oversee budgets and deadlines
To disguise poor communication	Help plan and diarise. Use electronic reminders
To live in a Pollyanna world where everything will be rosy	Don't let them live in a dream – point out how it affects you
To avoid responsibility and commitment	Discuss bottom lines and deal-breakers in your relationship with them
To avoid feelings of unhappiness	Not your problem
Others to take responsibility	Do not parent them

Chapter 9

Competitors

"She not only kept her lovely figure, she's added so much to it."
Bob Fosse

This group includes egomaniacs, boasters, tricksters, shysters, con-men and -women, and paranoids – and that's just the best of them. Competitors believe they can bludgeon their way through life using sheer willpower. Other people are regarded as opponents, obstacles or opportunities.

Great Competitors of history

- Julius Caesar
- Joan of Arc
- Alexander the Great
- Napoleon
- Lance Armstrong
- Louis IV.

How to spot a Competitor

It is possible to think of life as being a bit like a pie, and there are two ways of regarding it: big pie thinking and little pie thinking.

Big pie thinkers take the point of view that there is enough pie for everyone: "If you have a large slice that's great; I'd like a large slice as well." Little pie thinkers take the position that there is only so much pie to go around – supplies are limited: "If you have a large slice, that means less for me."

Competitors and other seriously self-obsessed types are little pie thinkers.

Insight is not the strongest suit of Competitors and the seriously self-obsessed. They are generally people of action rather than reflection. And victory isn't just a goal for these people – it is mandatory.

This means that they will get themselves into scrapes and battles that aren't worth fighting. Some will be confrontational just for the sake of it.

Diagnostic checklist for Competitors

- Will argue tooth and nail
- Will battle hammer and tongs
- Invest a lot of energy in frivolous battles
- Can be petty
- Are unscrupulous
- Are gleeful in victory
- May be boastful
- No self-esteem problems
- Believe that winning isn't an objective; winning is life
- Are not team players
- Have difficulty with collaboration
- Find it hard when others succeed
- Can't help but take the bait
- Focus on what they do right and what you do wrong
- May "find" crises when you are away to show that you are inept
- Are fearful of not being the best.

"Keep away from people who try to belittle your ambitions. Small people always do that, but the really great ones make you feel that you, too, can become great."

Mark Twain

Favourite phrases

- "How good am I?"
- "That's enough about you; let's talk about me."

The goal of their behaviour

Winning might seem the obvious goal of their behaviour, but it is actually not losing. Competitors and the seriously self-obsessed can't abide losing. For them, second place is a devastating place to be – it can be a huge blow to their self-esteem. They need to win constantly to relentlessly bolster their ego.

Key strategies

- Any cunning, conniving, tricky business that will ensure they win
- Some Competitors will select their battlegrounds very narrowly, and will not be prepared to engage in activities where the probability of complete victory is less than certain.

In the workplace

If you are working with Competitors, you may feel that you have been catapulted back in time to the days when you argued with your brothers or sisters. Many Competitors embark on an organisational version of sibling rivalry. They will vie with you over the most trivial issues in an attempt to elbow themselves ahead. Competitors usually take everything personally, too.

Some Competitors insist that special rules be made for them – they are an exception and deserve special treatment. Usually this "special treatment" involves them getting out of the mucky things everyone else is supposed to do.

One of the really infuriating things about these characters is, as Somerset Maugham observed, "If you refuse to accept anything but the very best, you will get it."

In workplaces, Competitors can hone their skills. Women who are Competitors may be more likely to focus on who is in and who is excluded from the "elite" club. Men who are Competitors may be more focused on who is further up the hierarchy, and how they can exert their power over those further down for their own benefit.

Tokens of status, such as your parking space, office position, the car you drive, and the clothes you wear, become incredibly important in workplaces with Competitors.

Aligned with these characteristics are the seriously self-obsessed personalities who plumb the depths of pettiness. They will do anything to gain an edge or advantage. But, as Lily Tomlin once observed, the only problem about the rat race is that, even if you win, you are still a rat.

If you are managing or leading these tricky people, issue challenges, set targets, set personal bests, establish roadmaps – keep them so busy and focused on getting ahead that they won't have time to engage in gloating, boasting and slicing up the opposition.

Celebrate achieving (or exceeding) milestones as a team. Don't get into the "most productive employee of the month" malarkey; the team should get the rewards. Awarding a single-minded, maniacal Competitor with individual recognition only demotivates everybody else.

Competitive managers are often very successful, so being associated with them can be good for your career. If you have a competitive boss, know that they will expect 110 percent commitment. Be punctual. Don't make excuses. Also know not to compete with them. Instead, contribute to their great glories.

If you have such a boss, you must always look totally engaged in the task at hand. Know how to look busy even if you aren't. One employee I know used to photocopy novels and bring them to work in an impressive folder. During quiet times, he would produce the folder and a highlighter, and could be seen reading through some "very important" documents.

There's only room for one in the limelight

I was supervised by someone with inferior qualifications to me. Sharsti was threatened by my presence because I knew I did a great job. The project I was running was very successful, and Sharsti began not communicating with me, giving other people the job of checking up on me – what time I started work, etc. She began to accuse me of things I hadn't done.

> At a peak time, she approved leave applications from my team against my wishes. Some colleagues stuck by me; others didn't, for fear of repercussions.
>
> Sharsti then set me up and accused me of making a serious mistake, and I was sacked. I was devastated. I took them to court for unfair dismissal and won my job back, but it was never the same. I ended up leaving anyway.

In your personal and social life

Competitors in families never end their battles. Year after year they return at times of family celebration to the hoary old battleground of their youth. It was here, in this very arena, that they first tasted that heady brew of victory. It was here, in the stadium known as "the family home", that they first cut their teeth as Competitors.

Now I ask you: what type of Competitor lets a home-ground advantage go to waste? And so we see the old battles loom – whose present was the biggest, who has the bigger income, who went on the most stylish holiday this year, who has the slimmest figure, who has the best sex life, or who is ageing the least? And on and on it goes – all completely unnecessary twaddle, of course.

It is only when you can recognise this game for what it is, and decide you don't have to win, that you can begin to enjoy it.

Inheritances

One of the big issues that infects people who share a family with a Competitor is inheritance. The common scenario is that a Competitor, in the months leading up to a relative's death, will move in under the pretext of having to give up their normal life to care for their ailing family member. Here the Competitor will employ methods usually reserved for martyrs and the High and Mighties. They will secretly ask the dying relative to sign over the rights to the house or money that should be equitably shared between family members, in order to "cover costs". Later they will reveal that this wasn't done with any thought of personal gain or profit, but to help the poor relative through their final days. Complete codswallop, of course.

It is sad that at a time when you may be grieving the loss of a loved one, you also have to keep a wary eye on a Competitor. But it is true. You will need to stay on your toes. Sadly, the best advice here is to remember that rats are most active in the darkest of hours.

Friendship with Competitors

Competitors don't form friendships so much as shaky, pragmatic alliances. The warm human bonding that occurs in the give-and-take of close friendship is really not for them. Of course, they like a few people around to provide an audience for their latest success. What is competition without a cheer squad, after all?

But "friendship" with Competitors can be vibrant fun. They are people who, when not involved in a vendetta, are full of the zing of life. A vitality for jousting with life oozes from their pores. But avoid entering into areas they are competitive about; otherwise they'll drop you like a bucket of hot coals.

Competitors and romance

Romance with Competitors can be beautiful. They will want to be your best lover, shower you with the most beautiful flowers and gifts, and love you more deeply, powerfully and truly than anyone who may have gone before. But if you want to remain the focus of a Competitor's desire, scarcity is the key. They enjoy the chase more than the catching, the challenge more than the conquest. As with High and Mighties, make yourself too available, and you will soon be a forgotten entry on their "To do" list. Remain flighty and elusive, and you'll have them in the palm of your hand.

> One example of a great rivalry occurred between Winston Churchill and the playwright George Bernard Shaw. Shaw invited Churchill to the first night of his new play, signing off with: "Bring a friend, if you have one." Churchill wrote back: "Impossible to be present for the first performance. Will attend the second – if there is one."

Tricky conversations with Competitors

- **R** Respond with respect
- **E** Engage
- **S** Seek understanding
- **O** Observe feelings
- **L** Lower the tone
- **V** Value-add
- **E** Empower

R Respond with respect

Some people use conversations to connect with other people and to build bridges of understanding. Others use them as one would a seesaw, where one person is "up" and the other one is definitely "down". Competitors belong to the second group.

The question is not whether there will be a competition, but where and when you want the competition to happen. You can delay the competition by practising advanced invisibility skills (see Chapter 5 on Bullies and Tyrants) for a time, but inevitably the contest will occur.

The reason for this is that any challenge to a Competitor is a threat to be squashed.

How much energy do you have to change their competitive behaviour? Remember, you only have so much time and energy to put into other people's competitions. Ignoring most of their behaviours and just getting on with things often makes more sense.

Half of successfully dealing with Competitors is deciding what not to get dragged into. Letting them focus on eliminating any sign of challenge from you, while you merrily get on with your life, can be quite satisfying.

It is also worthwhile considering the benefits of having a Competitor around – e.g., reducing your own workload. Competitors may insist on arranging social outings or family functions, and these will be the best functions, the most delicious dinner parties, the swishiest soirées.

What is not to like? Make a rule of never dissuading someone who really wants to be helpful.

As Abraham Lincoln observed, one of the best ways to lose an enemy is to make them into a friend.

Before responding and having a tricky conversation with Competitors, it is worth asking yourself a few serious questions:

- When people push, do you have to push back?
- What goads you into competition?
- Do you feel less able, or lose self-esteem, because of the Competitor's actions?
- Do they make you feel deflated?
- Do you end up fighting battles you don't want to have?
- Do you become locked into competing with them yourself?
- Do you give up or stop trying? Do you become subservient?

Reacting without thinking, rather than responding, means that you will end up playing on the Competitor's terms.

More than any other type of tricky person, the issues you may have with Competitors are influenced by your own style.

Based on your self-analysis in Chapter 2, Warriors can get all hot and bothered by Competitors and charge in, lance extended. Harrumphing and puffing, they get all heated up over slights and challenges.

Visionaries often feel slighted and misunderstood by Competitors. Visionaries can seriously underestimate their own level of competitiveness. "Competitive, moi?" they may ask innocently, as if winning never entered their creative heads. This can lead to them under-playing their hand. If you really want to win, sometimes you need to be honest about it and go for the outcome you are seeking.

Healers often want to appease and let the Competitor have their way. However, if Healers let Competitors make decisions that are socially or morally abhorrent to them, they can then fight hard. Healers compete indirectly through being nice. If that doesn't work, they appeal to moral authority.

Wise Ones may prepare their defence with the care of a barrister and then, sometimes, do nothing with it. They can risk being left behind by the energy and pace of Competitors. Nevertheless, Wise Ones are often shrewd, and may find the needle that will puncture the inflated ego of the Competitor.

It is easy to see Competitors as driven, rude, determined characters who are so set on victory that they will ride over anyone to get it. That's because they are. However, this also denies the fact that we are all Competitors. You come from a long line of Competitors. Your ancestors survived. Some of them learned to survive through brash boldness, others through social ways and charm.

Some things are worth competing for. Knowing how to prioritise and how to compete well is the trick.

 Engage

Collaboration rather than competition is an admirable goal. Live and let live; turn the other cheek; treat people as you would like to be treated – these are all marvellous concepts, but unless you are a master therapist, you will not be able to shift these tricky people's love of competition. Many Competitors are not going to respond to your suggestion of collaboration by thinking, "What a terrific idea; let's all pitch in together and reap the shared rewards!" Instead, many will think, "Fantastic! I've got a complete patsy on my hands. How far can I take this?"

The dilemma most of us face in dealing with Competitors is: "Do I get down and dirty in the gutter-fight, or do I remain true to my values and get railroaded in the process?" Essentially, is it better to be a highly principled pushover or a bare-fisted brawler? Do you put up with short-term defeat and hope that karma will take care of it later?

Fortunately, the choice is not so stark. Holding on to your core values and being true to them is important. Battles over family welfare, security and personal finances are worth winning. There are non-negotiables for us all.

 Seek understanding

Realise that competitiveness is an innate need for these people. They will spend their lives engaging in battles, skirmishes and squabbles they don't need. It is OK to be competitive under the right circumstances. The big difference is that they have very little, if any, choice over their competitive desires, whereas you have a choice. Knowing that their competitiveness is not entirely under their control helps us to not take things quite so personally.

 Observe feelings

You may find yourself replicating the way you related to your siblings when you deal with a Competitor. You may find yourself toppled back into the hurly-burly of childhood defeats and conquests. For example, competitive managers may push the very same buttons that were activated by your brothers and sisters. As a result, there is a risk that you may re-play earlier roles.

Oldest children may become frustrated and feel that their good efforts are overlooked by the Competitor. This may lead them to snipe about the Competitor to others or try harder to impress him or her.

Middle children may try to face the battle head-on and vie with the Competitor for attention.

Youngest children may try to use charm to bewitch the Competitor – a rarely successful strategy, unless you see yourself as someone's latest conquest – or else pull up stumps and leave the Competitor to play their own games.

Single children may be completely flummoxed by the Competitor's behaviour and feel overwhelmed.

 Lower the tone

Sometimes, if there is a battle to be fought, you should choose the time and place. The competition doesn't have to be brutal, and it doesn't have to usurp your own values.

Most Competitors are in a rush for the glory, so slow and steady is often the best tactic. Compete if you want to, but do so at your own pace. There are several stages to this:

1. **Dangle the bait.** Remember, Competitors have little choice but to compete. Place a challenge before them, and they are onto it with victorious glee. Of course, you needn't just place one challenge in front of them.
2. **Drop the rope.** As the world of Competitors is a do-or-die battle, the one strategy they don't expect is that you will simply give in.

You can't run a tug of war if one side refuses to pick up the rope. If your power base analysis (see Chapter 2) suggests you are weaker, your best strategy may be to surrender – or, even better, act as if the Competitor is part of your own team. Praise them. Encourage them. Delight in their successes. You do not have to choose to engage in their battle.

3. **Let them run themselves ragged.** Competitors generally have more energy to put into any battle than anyone else does. If you don't feel you have the interest or stamina to endure an intense competition, it may be better to pull out the deck chair, pour yourself a cool drink, and watch them frantically rush about.

4. **Hold true to your values and get on with the life you want to lead.**

 Value-add

If you put your mind to it, you can have a lot of fun with Competitors. Knowing that it rankles every time someone else shines is very helpful. Pointing out the positives in other people's accomplishments sends them into a frenzy.

One technique is called "poking around with a sharp stick". In this method, you highlight the skills, abilities and talents of others. Be overwhelmingly positive about someone. While you are not directly comparing them to the Competitor, this will have the latter frothing.

Competitors want to be thought of as the best. Remember the stepmother in Snow White?

> "Mirror, mirror on the wall
> Who is the fairest of them all?"

Before long they will be pacing the floor and cooking up the poisoned apples.

The eagerness of Competitors to be acknowledged as the best may even lead them to declare "I'm better than them!" Saying "Now, now, we know you are very good, but self-praise is no recommendation" won't help them to sleep easier at nights.

Don't torment Competitors too much, though – you may benefit from some of the things they do. An ego based intently on victory is an ego that can easily be crushed. Competitors feel disappointments and setbacks badly, so don't be too harsh with them. It may be more useful to you to praise their efforts rather than stifle them.

Commonly, people see Competitors as the enemy. In his wonderful *Inner Game* series of books, Timothy Gallway points out that it is preferable to see a Competitor as a friend who can help you learn how to play the game of life even better.

Some of the most powerful lessons we learn in life are taught to us by ferocious challengers.

Competitors help you learn how to play the game of life at full throttle – no half measures. They are gung-ho characters. They can also help you learn that you don't need to engage in battles for prizes you don't want.

You may even learn to shift the battleground. This can be good fun and can help you to be with Competitors without being drawn into their games.

E Empower

One of the reasons you may have been vulnerable to Competitors is that you like to achieve things. Inadvertently this has led you to take up unnecessary challenges.

While Competitors race around like enraged bulls, you can develop the sleight of hand of a matador. You don't need to get sucked into battles you don't have to fight. Avoiding, deflecting or, even more powerfully, agreeing with a Competitor's point of view has the effect of disarming them.

Just because they are competent doesn't mean you are any less able.

Competitors may suffer from the superman/superwoman syndrome. Men may claim to be the perfect husband, the world's greatest father, and the most glittering professional. Women may claim to have the brightest children, the best career, and an immaculate home as well as the perfect marriage. These people believe they can get their capes out, wear their underwear on the outside, and avoid the kryptonite.

They can achieve great leaps and bounds and churn out admirable achievements ... for a time. But these type-A characters are prone to burn-out, exhaustion and, if they are not careful, heart attacks.

Competitors can accomplish a lot but need to learn how to pace themselves. A consistent 80 percent effort may be better long term than a frantic 100 percent followed by a collapse. Watching them race around like ferrets on amphetamines will help you learn an essential life lesson: in the race between the hare and the tortoise, it's always better to be the tortoise.

Finally, avoid comparative thinking.

The imitating Competitor

I work with a woman I call "The Imitator". Every time someone in our department buys something new or even gets a new haircut, she has to do the same. She has no identity of her own.

It is so bad that when another woman in the department built a new house, the Imitator had to build one too. The Imitator's house is a small replica of the other woman's house. I mean replica – down to the knobs on the cabinets. The woman who has the big house won't even go to The Imitator's house because it's all too weird.

In the past, if the woman with the big house bought a little black dress, new shoes, or even got her hair dyed, The Imitator had to do the same thing. It's just unreal …

Recently, though, The Imitator has copied me. I have brown hair that I just cut short. The Imitator dyed her hair brown and cut it short. My husband drives a new Jeep, and the Imitator's husband just bought a Jeep …

> *"She was what we used to call a suicide blonde –*
> *dyed by her own hand."*
> Saul Bellow

Action steps: Competitors

What do they want?	How should I respond?
To build their own self-esteem	Calmly reassure them they are great no matter how successful they are
Constant praise	Tacit approval
Power hits	Just because they need power, it does not have to come at your cost – you can choose to give up power, or not
Adrenaline from constant challenges and success	Let them
To maintain narcissistic self	Tacit approval, but if they are difficult or causing distress, let them know you do not approve of their behaviour
Approval from others higher up the hierarchy	Provide approval and challenges
Awe from those lower in the pecking order	Praise their useful behaviour; ignore or do not engage in destructive competitions

MEMORABLE INSULTS

"I've had a perfectly wonderful evening. But this wasn't it."

Groucho Marx

"Some cause happiness wherever they go; others, whenever they go."

Oscar Wilde

Chapter 10
Poor Communicators

"He may look like an idiot and talk like an idiot, but don't let that fool you. He really is an idiot."

Groucho Marx

Poor Communicators of history
- Reverend Spooner
- Ronald Reagan
- George W. Bush.

How to spot a Poor Communicator

Most of you will have been bailed up at a barbecue by someone who seems intent on informing you at length about the features of their car, or the obscure but fascinating theory they have about cement drying. They ignore your polite, subtle attempts to escape ("Well, I must get another drink" or "Oh dear, is that the time?") and corner you. Even the toilet provides only temporary refuge – they are waiting to continue the "discussion". At times like these your eyes wander around the room, looking for a saviour to interrupt, but they are all too savvy. In desperation, you gaze longingly at the pickled onions, wondering whether swallowing a whole one and inducing a medical emergency would be preferable to wasting your life hearing this drivel.

Welcome to the world of the Poor Communicator!

This group contains bores, drones, the obsessively fixated, thoughtless foot-in-mouth artists, dinner guests who won't leave, hotheads, verbal-diarrhoea dispensers, and the slyly secretive, who can empty most rooms in a fragment of a conversation. Subtlety is not their strong point.

Some university departments and public service organisations abound in these characters. Don't take it personally – most of them are equal-opportunity drongos who pay out on everyone.

Diagnostic checklist for Poor Communicators

- Are blustering loose cannons
- Are irrational and erratic
- Erupt without a moment's notice
- Have foot-in-mouth syndrome
- May play the martyr – let pressure build up and don't tell anyone about it until it is too late
- Prattle and drivel
- Are unpredictable/moody
- Will purge and complain at 100 kph without drawing breath
- Ride a roller coaster of emotions
- May be so vague and indirect you have no idea what they want
- Are confrontational
- Feel anxious about not being able to contain feelings.

Favourite phrases

- "Can I be brutally honest with you for a moment?"
- Qualifying any piece of praise with a "BUT ..."

The goal of their behaviour

Continuous talking may be a method of coping with social anxiety. As well as those who drone on, there are other Poor Communicators who use heat to cover up for a lack of substance. These are the dummy-spitters who can't express their feelings, so instead they chuck a wobbly, throw a tantie, or have a hissy fit. Both groups lack experience in the broader areas of life.

The goal of their behaviour is to cover up poor social and empathy skills. They have low emotional intelligence. They will talk the hind leg off a dog rather than show anyone else they are ill at ease. They read other people poorly. They may not realise that topics they find fascinating bore the pants off most people.

Key strategies

- Use put-downs as humour
- If slighted, become unforgiving
- Are insensitive
- Take over personal space and property
- Discuss offensive matters
- Turn conversations into dissertations on themselves
- Can be verbally abusive
- Ask probing questions and don't know when to stop.

In the workplace

Working with Poor Communicators is full of surprises. They won't give you the lead-in or the warning signs that other people give you. They play their cards very close to their chest.

Some bottle up frustrations and stress until they leap out like a frog's tongue after a fly. Being volatile, Poor Communicators can turn on you. These can be the hotheads that go from zero to one hundred just like that. The first time you experience this may be upsetting. The yelling, the wild look in their eyes, and perhaps the frothing at the mouth can look quite fearsome.

It's all a display that they have in the past used to get their own way.

If they explode, don't it take personally (even though they will be making personal accusations) and don't say much as all. Batten down your hatches and wait for the hurricane to blow itself out. If it all gets too much for you, stand up and silently walk away. If they yell at you to come back, keep walking.

Other Poor Communicators simply choose not to communicate. Your cheery "Good morning" is met with an Easter Island face. This can be particularly galling if they are chatty to others. You might have some fun by attempting to increase the exuberance of your greeting every day. See if you can make them crack. I have had absolutely no success whatsoever with this technique, but I've had a lot of fun trying.

Related to this group are the sly, secretive withholders of information. They are Poor Communicators who gain power through being in the know and leaving you in the dark. This often combines with being a Back-stabber as well.

Sad and even more onerous are those Poor Communicators who use a hundred words when two would do. These bores use any question as an opportunity to drill knowledge into you. You will know how the current weather relates to their second cousin on their mother's side's recovery from a hip replacement with complications. Around these Poor Communicators it is wise to become very focused. Concentrate your energies on a single outcome and use your energies to achieve that result.

Other Poor Communicators have ears but little ability to use them for listening. They pretend to listen but really have limited attention, so messages become skew-whiff. Rather than listening, they assume. They go off on a tangent and get the wrong end of the stick.

If you are managing or leading Poor Communicators, call them into your office regularly and ask them for their appraisal of any issues they have. Be proactive and try to get their gripes out into the open.

Shrewd leaders and managers can use Poor Communicators to gauge the market response to a new idea: Poor Communicators can rarely keep information to themselves and are legendary for delivering feedback bluntly. So they can provide bosses with a litmus test of how well a new initiative is being understood.

If one is your boss, watch him closely. Practise hawk-like observation skills. Try to know, even before he does, when he is having a bad day. If self-awareness is not the strong suit of tricky people generally, this is especially true for Poor Communicators. They are a total mystery to themselves.

Some poor-communicating managers are loose cannons that explode without warning; others are so indirect, casual, chit-chatting and vague that you end up not really having any idea at all what they want you to do.

The problem is, no one thinks they are a Poor Communicator. Your boss probably sincerely believes that he has clearly transmitted his wishes. If you don't check that you have a mutual understanding, you are sure to get it wrong.

In your personal and social life

You may encounter Poor Communicators who suffer from verbal diarrhoea – overly detailed descriptions that drive listeners barmy, such as: "Was it Monday? No, it was Tuesday. No, it must have been Monday because that was when my cat vomited …" Others repeat the same stories over and over again.

Then there are the thread-losers, who suffer from circumlocutory verbosity. Conversations with them are an indirect ramble across any topic that flits into their addled mind, with no relevance whatsoever to the matter at hand.

Some Poor Communicators have mastered the art of the useless discussion. These conspiring time-wasters tell you in great detail about something that someone has done, only to then either refuse to name names or forbid you to tell anyone else about the problem.

Poor Communicators and romance

Romantically, many a woman has partnered up with a man who is a Poor Communicator on the basis that still waters must certainly run deep, mistaking that silent brooding for the dark, beating heart of a complex poet – only to later discover that still waters sometimes don't run at all.

Silence kills more relationships than anger or betrayal does. If that mumbling, bumbling, incoherent romantic partner is starting to bore you, it's time to call it a day and move on. The likelihood of him developing a dazzling line of repartee and wit is zilch.

Most women have probably felt at times that their face was located somewhere in the vicinity of their cleavage: Poor Communicators may avoid eye contact, and instead prefer to focus on your chest.

Romantically being with someone who is so timid that he appears to have taken a vow of silence, or so chatty that he should have his own radio talkback show, can get a bit wearing. While it is worth trying to implement strategies to change the situation, communication is an area where you are either compatible or you are not. If a romantic partner's communication style begins to grate, it is often a death knell for the relationship.

Tricky conversations with Poor Communicators

- **R** Respond with respect
- **E** Engage
- **S** Seek understanding
- **O** Observe feelings
- **L** Lower the tone
- **V** Value-add
- **E** Empower

R Respond with respect

With poor communicators you may not have a lot of choice about preparing your initial response. Before you really know it, they are either bombarding you with a whirlwind of words or brooding silently and leaving you tiptoeing around, waiting for the eruption. Usually, the art of tricky conversations is perfected over time.

Deciding to intervene with a Poor Communicator who is unaware that he may be the source of trouble may well boil up a pot that is not worth boiling. Also, if he is as poor a communicator as you think he is, he may well be self-sabotaging already. As Napoleon once said, never interrupt your enemy while he is making a mistake.

So, there may not be an issue – unless, of course, he is in a position of power, seems unlikely to shift, or is maligning you personally.

Then taking action seems inevitable.

In all likelihood, you've had to put up with some absolute dunderheads at times. What have you tended to do? Zip your lip and play dead? Rear up like a wild banshee? Laugh off an absolute clanger? Ignore the slight and get on with your life? If you have tended to put up with it and seethe later, you may well have put up with too much.

One woman at a cocktail party approached another and said, "Congratulations! You're pregnant!", only to be told that the other woman had merely put on some weight. She made the same error that evening with three different women.

Most people are far too polite around Poor Communicators. Continuing to converse with someone who makes you feel you'd rather be conducting a self-appendicectomy through your nostrils is a stoic act. Rather than waiting for an opportune moment in an endless diatribe, a rapid but cheery "Sorry, must rush!" may save you endless hours.

Can you think of any times you have promptly identified Poor Communicators and moved swiftly on?

Based on the analysis in Chapter 2, Warriors tend to tackle Poor Communicators head-on, and in the process may turn a valuable ally into an arch-enemy. Generally, Poor Communicators don't change their ways after confrontation – mostly because they don't know how to. The more reflective among them become more subdued and less intrusive; the worst just get sulky and plot revenge.

Visionaries tend to glide over slights and barbed comments, only to later worry about them. By avoiding or ignoring the issue at the time, they can create great stress for themselves.

Healers want to appease Poor Communicators. They may apologise or excuse the poor communication to others: "Well, she doesn't really mean it" or "That's just his way; we all get used to it eventually."

Wise Ones think about how to use the Poor Communicator's coarseness and gaucheness for their own purposes.

Too many of us politely nod and allow ourselves to get caught up in the drivel because of courtesy. We may feel awkward about ending a conversation even though we know we should. This of course leads to later feeling annoyed that our precious social time was wasted.

 **Engage**

In all of our relationships we have four basic choices:

1. Stay in the relationship and change what can be changed and live by our values
2. Stay and accept what can't be changed and live by our values
3. Stay, give up, and do things that make the relationship worse
4. Leave the relationship and live by our values.

With Poor Communicators it important to remain true to your standards and not be tempted to slip down to the level of their sometimes-appalling practices.

Aim for dignity and courtesy. If you can't create these qualities in them, at least maintain them for yourself. This requires a personal code of conduct. Act in ways that allow you to be proud of yourself.

Assist Poor Communicators to develop clear, concise communication. Use emails or texting for some communication. If a verbal encounter is needed, make it time-limited by saying, "Unfortunately, I've only got five minutes now, but you've got my undivided attention for that time." At the end of five minutes, leave.

If your Poor Communicator is a droning, fixated bore, try to help him realise that others have different interests and aspirations. This may require you to be more brash than usual in discussions and to cut him off mid-stream by changing topics: "Oh, that reminds me, did you hear about …" or even "I'm sorry, but I couldn't be less interested in how a car's differential works."

 Seek understanding

Most Poor Communicators have no idea what they do – many think they are exemplary communicators. This means the problem is apparent to everyone except them. They may have a gob-smacking lack of insight. For instance, one manager whose conversational drudgery was making her staff feel that they would prefer to trim their toenails with a chainsaw announced loudly to all around that she was an expert in human relations with exceptional emotional intelligence.

 Observe feelings

The origins of poor communication include never having realised that other people may feel or think differently than the Poor Communicator does, or a family history of being overlooked and not heard, or a childhood of indulgence in which no one ever told them to stop. Regardless of the causes, there is a blurring of the Poor Communicator's boundaries between self and others.

Poor Communicators are not self-aware but are usually not malicious. They are doing this because they are unaware of social cues and are trying to make friends the best way they can. Don't take it personally.

Nevertheless, tricky conversations with them will require you to be more direct than you may usually be.

Curtail long-winded conversations with Poor Communicators by saying: "That's fascinating. Could you summarise that for me, so I can tell a friend?"

At the start of a conversation, say: "I've only got a minute and I need to do something soon." Be strict about leaving when the time is up.

Another ploy with Poor Communicators is to say: "This is so interesting, but you will have to tell me later. Could you please email me something about it?"

 Lower the tone

Another method for abbreviating tricky conversations with Poor Communicators is to pretend your mobile phone rang or, if they are on a mobile, claim that that their signal is breaking up. You could even set your phone alarm for two-minute intervals and answer the alarm.

If you need to ask a Poor Communicator for information, wait until they are seated. Remain standing yourself – you always need to be able to make a rapid getaway.

They may ask personal questions that are none of their business or assume you are close friends when you are not. Clarify the boundaries with them. Be prepared to say things like: "That's not really the issue right now" or "That's not appropriate in this setting."

Some Poor Communicators will confront you with an explosive barrage of undeserved abuse. Often in these situations it is best to stand strong, firm and silent. Sniping back at them just prolongs their attack. If a pause occurs, then calmly say: "I can see you're angry at the moment. Let's talk about this again when you are calmer." Then leave. If they pursue you, refuse to engage in further discussion.

Value-add

Realise that Poor Communicators find social situations anxiety-provoking. They are often much more stressed than you are. Behind their gauche, awkward ways are often people who feel quite isolated and afraid.

Get them used to your technique of kindly finishing a conversation. Become known to them as a person who does not engage in idle chit-chat. Be fiercely focused. Your time is limited, and there is only a limited supply of your life's energy.

Above all, as mentioned, don't take it personally. Some Poor Communicators can say the most dreadful, hurtful, mindless things. If you take these to heart, you'll be losing sleep in no time and on your way to regular courses of sedatives.

> *"You look into his eyes, and you get the feeling someone else is driving."*
>
> David Letterman

 Empower

One of the reasons you may have been vulnerable to Poor Communicators is that you are a good, attentive listener. You are polite and you are nice. Inadvertently this has led you to tolerate communication styles that are draining.

Poor Communicators teach us a number of useful skills for life. They can help us to strengthen ourselves against torrents of abuse. They can help us learn not to take things personally. They can help us to sharpen the clarity of our own communication.

Develop security shields for yourself so that you don't take offence. One useful way of doing this is to see an angry person as poisoned by something. While he is carrying on, you might like to silently speculate on what might have poisoned him and caused him this level of suffering. This shifts the question from "Why are they doing this to me?" to "I wonder what happened to this person for them to be acting in this way?"

Poor communicators also help us to value our own time. Being prepared to use time-efficient forms of communication and to be assertive about ending conversations is a useful talent.

You can also perfect the high-impact SWAT team approach. This is the fine art of the dash-and-grab conversation, where you whip in, say what you need to say, and are out of there before they really know what has struck them.

You can also develop your ability to manoeuvre conversations skilfully by practising changing subjects. It can be quite challenging to count how many topic changes you are able to create in a single interaction.

Poor Communicators also help us to learn the fine art of positioning. Where you place yourself at a social function, work meeting, or dinner party matters. Look for power positions where you have access to a range of people (and therefore conversational possibilities).

Don't allow yourself to be cornered or trapped.

You might also learn the importance of empathy and of reading cues in social situations.

Finally, Poor Communicators teach us that we can be strong. If need be, you can always walk away.

Ten tips for guests who won't leave

1. Check that they haven't confused your hospitable home with a boarding house.
2. Act as if you are the one leaving. Stand up and say, "It was wonderful having you here. We must do this again soon."
3. Tell them you aren't set up to host someone for longer than they have already been there. Be firm. If they are friends, they'll be packing right away. If they are leeches or freeloaders, they'll argue, beg and lay guilt trips on you to let them stay. Be firm, or they'll be there for months.
4. Play obnoxious music – loud. I always find rap music to be great for this, but it depends on the age and attitude of the guest.
5. Turn the lights up. Disconnect the electricity or gas. Set off the fire alarm.

6. Say: "Here, let me heat you up some leftovers. I'll put them in a takeaway container for you."
7. Even good guests can't mind-read. Say: "It's been a great night, but I have to sleep. Thanks for coming."
8. Pretend to fall asleep.
9. Confide in a good friend and ask him or her to go around telling everyone goodnight, mentioning the time and how tired everyone seems.
10. Put your pyjamas on and let people know you are heading for bed.

Action steps: Poor Communicators

What do they want?	How should I respond?
To cope with anxiety in social situations	Be brief, kind and affirming
To manage frustrations	Clear talk when you are calmer
To make friends and influence others (albeit with poor social skills)	Be friendly, encouraging and move on
They are genuinely interested in topics such as train timetables that are deadly boring to others; they have a need to convey their enthusiasm and knowledge	Say: "That's fascinating – would you mind sending me an email about it? I have to go now"

MEMORABLE INSULTS

"He has Van Gogh's ear for music. "

Billy Wilder

"In order to avoid being called a flirt, she always yielded easily"

Charles, Count Talleyrand

Part 2

Help for everyone – including tricky people

"If it wasn't for me, I would do brilliantly."
Jean Chamfort

Chapter 11
If the tricky person in your life is you

Yikes! You've read this book with a wry nod – "Yeah, I've done that." Perhaps you've even identified yourself as a tricky person.

Sometimes we can plainly see in others what we fail to see in ourselves. Our ability to detect cowardice, pride, vanity, miserliness, egotism or uber-controlling acts in others may belie these qualities in us.

Well, there are benefits as well as costs to being a tricky person. Many of the tricky behaviours described in this book exist because they work. Generally they work to conceal lowered self-esteem, feelings of insecurity, fears of inadequacy, anxiety, and feelings of powerlessness. These are feelings that all humans have occasionally. Inevitably, we all act in tricky ways, especially when we feel threatened.

Tricky behaviours may help you to get your own way, but they come with a cost. The cost is a loss of intimacy. People find it harder to be close to or love tricky people. Subtly, friendships become more distant, romances sour, families becomes less communicative, and work becomes less collegial.

Tricky people may be proud of their accomplishments but may not like themselves so much. They may be able, for a short time, to get other people to do what they want. Long term, however, this is rarely effective.

Almost everyone wants intimacy. When people were surveyed about what they would do if they had an additional three hours a day to spend as they wished, overwhelmingly they said they would spend more time with friends and family.

> "A narcissist is someone better looking than you are."
> Gore Vidal

If you would like to have more intimacy in your life, you will need to give up your tricky ways. There are several steps towards doing this:

1. **Identify your pattern of relating to others.**
2. **Give up that response for a minimum of six weeks.**
   - If back-stabbing has been your thing, don't say a bad word about anyone for six weeks.
   - If blaming and whinging has been your game, make no complaints about anyone or anything for six weeks. Whatever happens, take responsibility.
   - If bullying and tyranny have been part of your repertoire, let people be who they are in the way they wish to be. Ban sarcasm, insults, and any other personal comments that are negative, even if they do seem funny to you.
   - If you have been controlling, don't steer others. Practise the art of listening to others without judging, blaming or fixing. Practise the art of accepting life as it shows up.
   - If you have been High and Mighty, applaud others, admire people, and be gracious. Refuse to make "helpful" suggestions to others in order to "improve things" for them. Let people make their own choices.
   - If you have been an Avoider, no ducking, weaving, hiding, lying or prevaricating for six long, direct weeks.
   - If you have been a vehement Competitor, don't turn issues into a win/loss situation, and allow others to "win" for six long, humble weeks.

- If you are a Poor Communicator, practise listening for six weeks. Listening means hearing and understanding, not just waiting for the other person to stop speaking so you can say something.

Of course, in those six weeks you will have relapses. Your patterns are well worn and hard to shake off. Even so, persist. Observe yourself and be as aware as you can be of not slipping back into old habits.

3. **Give to other people what you wish to receive for yourself.**

    If you want more friendship, give your friendship to other people. If you want to feel more loved, be more loving towards others. If respect is what you want, give other people more respect. One of the great lessons that human life has for us is that we generally get back what we give out.

> **Learning to live with myself**
>
> My family is packed to the rafters with tricky characters, and I used to be awful. Instead of deciding to live my own life, I blamed my family for every low-down, sneaky act that I committed. I lauded it over friends; I railroaded dates into more intimacy than they wanted; I used underhand tactics to gain an edge at work. I had an encyclopedia of excuses designed to get out of any situation.
>
> When I acted like that, what surprised me was that most people were too polite to ever challenge me. They'd give in all the time, so I thought I was winning. Deep down, though, I wasn't happy. I detested myself; I felt like a fraud. I didn't have friends – I had captives.
>
> I decided to create a "me" that I could live with, to become someone I could like. I didn't realise how hard this was going to be. I was addicted to cheating, to being sneaky, lying and self-serving. But slowly, over time, I changed my ways: I stopped lying, I banned myself from making excuses, and I stopped trying to get other people to always do what I wanted. And after all that, I gradually began to actually respect other people.

There are costs, of course. I don't get my way all the time now, and that's taken some getting used to. On the upside, though, I really like myself for the first time in my life, so it's been worth it.

MEMORABLE INSULTS

"Why do you sit there looking like an envelope without any address on it?"

Mark Twain

"I have never killed a man, but I have read many obituaries with great pleasure."

Clarence Darrow

Chapter 12
Workplace politics – a survival guide

Workplaces can be very, very happy places to be, but when they go wrong they usually manage to do so in soul-destroying ways.

In the seething cesspit of the office or workplace, all kinds of tricky people can thrive. Take a good, long, hard look at your colleagues and workmates.

- Who is bossing someone else around by taking the high moral ground?
- Who is on a mission with a maniacal, competitive look and a take-no-prisoners attitude?
- Who cowers in their cubicle like a beaten animal, licking their wounds?
- Who conspires with other plotters to bring down the empire?
- Who is the anti-personnel officer?

The law of the jungle prevails. Many workplaces contain dominance hierarchies that would put a pack of squabbling hyenas to shame. For the babe in the woods, there are a few basic tips for survival.

Before sharing these, let's take the focus up-close and personal. Never forget that what seems like a lovable rascal from a distance can be a real pain close up. Your response depends on your proximity to him.

It was my first real job, in a government department, doing what seemed initially to be important things. There were four of us in the team; at least, that is what the organisational chart suggested.

To my left sat Hamish, a wizened man whose sole occupational achievement, as far as I could discern, was to shape a forest of bonsai plants on his desk. To my right lay Jackie, a young woman who suffered from the alphabet. She had CFS (chronic fatigue syndrome), RSI (repetitive strain injury), and other letters of the alphabet as well. Jackie appeared every morning with a different part of her body in a padded brace and felt the need to spend the day lying under her desk. Jackie snored.

Glancing at my co-workers, I had the sneaking suspicion that if any work was going to be done, it was going to be up to me. So, with some hope for support, I gazed in the direction of my team leader.

His desk was meticulously neat and always uncluttered by human presence until 10.30 a.m. Clive would arrive every day with considerable ceremony in a waft of after-shave and with his phone pinned to his ear. He would spend five intense minutes barking instructions and checking the progress made towards our mission statement by us lesser mortals before leaving on an essential errand.

I never learned exactly what important task called Clive away from his desk during these vital times but, whatever it was, it required him to drink a lot of alcohol. He would return as plastered as the walls, but promptly, at 2.30 p.m. Swaying like a mound of jelly in an earthquake, he would then write on the whiteboard his hopes and dreams for a retirement package. He wrote:

"Clive wants a package."

Then he would leave for the day. Eventually they promoted Clive.

Now those of you who are suffering the blowtorch of workplace politics may say this is pretty mild stuff. I'd be inclined to agree with you. I was only surrounded by total cot-cases. It was a sheltered workshop for the intellectually able.

For those of you facing a seemingly endless stream of tricky conversations in a confined area with Bullies, Tyrants, Controllers, Avoiders and Back-stabbers, my heart goes out to you. Let's see if we can create a few guidelines to help you survive.

1. **In any workplace, the person who has the most options is also the person with the most power.** For example, those who feel able to leave, if they were to decide to do so, have more power than those who feel trapped or unable to leave because of poor job prospects. Those who have more control over their work have more power than those who do not. Therefore, it is always desirable in a workplace to try, over time, to increase the options you have.

2. **Pessimists are the people who have most to lose.** Look around any meeting – the person who is most pessimistic about any new proposal will be the possessor of power. That is because change represents a threat to their power. This is helpful to know in analysing who has real power over different issues, and can also help you to understand why some very well-thought-out initiatives are never adopted.

3. **When a new boss arrives, all bets are off.** Even if you feel you understand how the politics work, as soon as a new manager takes on the job, the set roles will spill. This is why a new management team represents a golden opportunity to re-shuffle the pecking order.

4. **Meetings can be productive and fun.** This is very important. Some meetings are forums for time-wasting at best, and for someone to self-aggrandise at worst. Despite this, many organisations love holding meetings. Converting long-winded meetings into fun may seem difficult, but it's not impossible.

   One job I had involved interminable meetings, so a few of us decided to liven them up. We would choose a word for the meeting, and hold a fierce competition to be the first to insert that word or phrase into the meeting in a semi-logical way. The meetings that involved the words "turmeric" and "asparagus" stand out as particularly memorable. Comments like "The plan has a whiff of turmeric about it" and "The proposal is about as limp as a piece of old asparagus" perplexed most of the attendees but gave a few of us no end of fun.

5. **The biggest protection against office politics that you have long-term is to be an exemplary performer.** So, get to know the four rules of exemplary performance:

    Rule 1: Anything is possible.
    Rule 2: Nothing is easy.
    Rule 3: When things are easy, be grateful.
    Rule 4: When things are difficult, remember Rule 1.

6. **Know how to thrive, not just survive, at work.**

    Fergus O'Connor, in his wonderful book *How to Do a Great Job and Go Home on Time*, has some great ideas for thriving at work. These include:

    - Prioritise every day. Ask yourself: "If I could only do one thing today, what would it be?"
    - Make a plan for the next day last thing before you go home.
    - Do one thing at a time and finish it – don't faff about.
    - Come in early and leave early (but make sure you do leave early!).
    - Use "red time" and "green time" if you can – "green time" means you can be interrupted; "red time" means you have to focus.
    - Use email and voice messages to avoid meetings.
    - Remember that nobody ever got promoted for keeping an empty inbox.

Managing your board – a guide for bosses and leaders

Boards and councils are never neutral – someone has selected them. Read them carefully and well. Always keep analysing who is for you, who is against you, and who is neutral. Keenly attend to their interests, preferences and biases.

Don't always speak your mind. Hear others' opinions about an issue first before declaring a position.

Never put a proposal to a meeting if you don't have the numbers. Lobby first, then take the issue to the board. If you don't have the numbers over critical issues, plea-bargain with key board members (e.g., "I really need you on my side on this issue").

Separate governance and operations. Some boards want to meddle in operational decisions, so it is vital to delineate the boundaries of interest and responsibility.

Have one person permanently chairing the meetings. It is a skilled position, and much power resides in the chair. Rotating chairs are only useful when the person holding the chair is doing it poorly. Try not to chair yourself.

Work to board members' strengths. Try to guess the question they are most likely to ask, and try to answer it before they have asked it.

Go head-hunting for allies – cultivate allegiances with key board members. When the board wants you to take a particular course of action, ask yourself two questions:

1. Do I have to do it?
2. Do I have to do it now?

Trust your hunches. If you have a strong hunch but everyone disagrees, stall for time.

Make yourself and your achievements shine

Try to put most of your energies into high-importance/high-visibility activities. Some activities in life are like cleaning bathrooms; they are only noticed when they are not done. Always remember the 80/20 principle: 80 percent of your impact comes from 20 percent of what you do.

		Importance	
		High	Low
Urgency	High	Do it	Delegate it
	Low	Diarise it	Delight in it or don't do it

Here are some more tips:

- Be the populist of your organisation: give the people what they want, when they want it, where they want it, and in a way they can use it.
- Think about what people might need and try to provide it.
- Don't tell others about your achievements; let your actions speak for you.
- Analyse your strengths and leverage these.
- Never seem to be working too hard. It's better to appear to be a genius than a workaholic.
- Foster a calm, unflustered style.
- Creating a distinctive style draws positive attention to you. Try to be the most interesting person in the room.
- Don't criticise others – ever.
- Adapt your style to the person you are with. The idea that one size fits all does not work if you want to be successful.
- Make small requests of others for assistance. People like to be consistent, so if they help you once there is a tendency for them to want to help you in the future. Always make sure your requests are easy for people to do, and always express gratitude. Never ask for big favours.
- Be friendly but not over-familiar with bosses.
- Don't be the bearer of bad news.
- Be enthusiastic and positive.
- Never, ever make jokes about people's appearance (weight, haircuts, style).
- Don't gossip – everyone tells at least one other person.
- Try to exceed expectations.

> *"She plunged into a sea of platitudes, and with the powerful breaststroke of a Channel swimmer, made her confident way towards the white cliffs of the obvious."*
> W. Somerset Maugham

Great performance appraisals

- "His team will follow him anywhere ... but only out of curiosity."
- "He has carried out each and every one of his duties to his entire satisfaction."
- "He would be out of his depth in a car-park puddle."
- "This young lady has delusions of adequacy."
- "Since my last report, he has reached rock bottom and has started to dig."
- "She sets low personal standards and then consistently fails to achieve them."
- "He has the wisdom of youth, and the energy of old age."
- "Works well when under constant supervision and cornered like a rat in a trap."
- "The gates are down, the lights are flashing, but the train isn't coming."
- "So dense, light bends around him."
- "The wheel is turning, but the hamster is dead."

Chapter 13
Tricky conversations and relationship patterns

This book is all about relationships when they become tricky. They may become tricky in families, in marriage, at work, in the social world, or in romance.

Once a relationship becomes tricky, it often stays that way, partly because the relationships we have with each other follow patterns, and changing these patterns can be more difficult than de-spotting an angry leopard.

We can identify the different types of tricky people we meet and start to develop strategies for coping with them, but sometimes we need to go further. In tricky relationships there are two people: the tricky person and ourselves (who may or may not be doing things in our own quirky, tricky way).

There are two basic patterns in relationships: see-saws and escalators. See-saw relationships occur when one person takes on a role and the other takes on a complementary role – for example, one up–one down, persecutor–victim or distancer–pursuer. Escalator relationships happen when both people take on similar roles – for example, as arch-rivals or competitors.

See-saw and escalator relationships feel different for those in them, and require different strategies to alter the basic patterns.

Before we look at both patterns, let's lift the veil on this business of relationships and see if we can discern the cogs that are grinding and the wheels that are spinning behind the scenes.

Attraction

Firstly, with the exception of family members, we don't end up in relationships with most of the people in our lives by accident. Either we choose them or they choose us, or we both choose one another. It's a matter of choice.

You might airily tell me that you and your friend/manager/business partner/lover/husband/wife met at a party and something "just clicked". Let's look at what caused that "click" to occur. What starts most relationships is attraction. Even in a work setting, you were attracted to the idea of working there.

Attraction is not a matter of accident, but it's not a matter of conscious choice, either. Often we become attracted to people who appear to have handled things that we find difficult to deal with. In a sense, part of attraction is solving a problem – we look for people who are capable in areas where we feel vulnerable. For example, a woman who grows up in an alcoholic family may select someone who is as dry as a Methodist christening. A man who has grown up in harsh or violent circumstances may search for a partner who is as peaceful as Mother Teresa.

And so there the world should live happily ever after, right? Wrong! Dead wrong!

The shadow self

As all of us grow up, there are parts of ourselves that people praise and find acceptable. "He's so good at …", "I love the way you …", "She's such a clever girl – see how she …", and "Aren't you wonderful at …" are some of the phrases that indicate to us that these are desirable characteristics. And they shouldn't just be applauded – these characteristics should, we feel, be put on display, because on display they will gain us love and accolades.

But we are not just dancing seals performing for the next bit of fish; we also put on display those parts of ourselves that we value.

For almost every characteristic that we put on show, there are others that have not been approved of or applauded. There are the parts of ourselves that we don't like so much. Without really thinking about it, we shove these parts under the carpet. After a while we become so good at this, we can even pretend they never existed at all. These parts are known as "the shadow self".

We go out into the world in search of people to relate to. Without really meaning to, we seek out others who appear to be capable in areas in which we feel vulnerable. The only problem here is that what gives them the appearance of being capable is, often, that they have tucked away and hidden the very same stuff that you find difficult to deal with. They may even have a better disguise than the one you have.

What do shadow selves do?

This shadow self is not an entirely controllable beast. It slips off the leash and gets out of the cage in times of duress and stress. It loves bad-hair days. Someone, for example, who has selected a mild-mannered, placid soul to be with, may find that in difficult times this partner can become a seething vat of fury and rage. A shy, retiring person who has found a wild party gal or guy as a partner may be dismayed when the latter becomes a mild homebody or a workaholic.

This partly explains why relationships can begin with the sense that "we have so much in common", only to find crevasses of difference later on. The people haven't actually changed, but their shadow selves have come out to play.

Before thinking about other people's shadows, it is always worth acknowledging your own. Shadow selves gain power when people pretend they don't exist. The first part of helping yourself with this is to look for parts of yourself that you don't like, and accept that they are there. Accepting yourself warts and all is a first step in this. Accepting doesn't mean excusing yourself for every nasty, mean, sneaky, cranky thing you've done; it means acknowledging that at times you can be like this.

Accepting that others also have shadows that they are largely unaware of can help you to understand their behaviour, even if you don't like it.

It is very useful to be aware of and be able to observe shadows when they arise.

A word of caution: don't point out someone else's shadow to them. In the heat of an argument it can be awfully tempting to tell someone "You always do ... and I know exactly why! It's because you can't handle ..." Don't do this! People have spent years carefully assembling a self that conceals the shadow parts of themselves, so if you point this out to them when they are upset or angry, they will argue that you are wrong, and may even become violent.

> "When I accept others as they are
> Then they can change
> When I accept myself for who I am
> Then I can change"
> Carl Rogers

The fine balance of security and freedom

Shadow selves don't just play a role in attraction, they also impact on the fine checks and balances that play out in many relationships, which often involve a trade-off between security and freedom. The security of continuity, reliability and monogamy is often balanced with sacrificed individual freedoms.

If the basic trade-off is between security and freedom, it is often an unspoken one. Love is not tangible, nor is it necessarily binding. It may last a lifetime, a few years or weeks, or merely days. So we seek out solid forms of proof of love.

These trade-offs can lead to tricky conversations. As people try to guarantee security, they can engage in behaviour that is designed to dominate others. Those who try to escape being dominated may engage in avoidant and elusive behaviours to ensure their freedom.

Biologically, the balance between security and freedom has been at the basis of survival. The continuation of the species has relied on a delicate balance between the vulnerability of the mother and child, and the certainty of paternity.

In child development, there are vast advantages for babies if they look like their father. This similarity of appearance is important for the child's survival and bonding, which primarily rely on the security of the mother. When there is anxiety about a lack of security, we see surges in postnatal depression. When there is insecurity in families, it often shows up in the behaviour of children.

This isn't restricted to those raising children. As relationships develop and mature, imperatives shift. Part of the mid-life crisis may be simply that, biologically speaking, the job is done. If there is security to be sought then, it is in having your family look after you in your old age.

In same-sex as well as heterosexual relationships, both partners may become anxious about the effects of time's passing on their physique and appearance, and begin to fear they may be traded in for a newer, fresher model.

Security and freedom are often seen as mutually exclusive. One threatens stability; the other threatens growth. In truth they can be compatible. Security delivers the freedom to do other things in life beyond mere survival and continuation of the species. Conversely, security concerns lead to increased anxiety and a retraction of freedoms. We see this vividly in abuses of privacy and human rights in times of war and conflict.

How to be secure and free is part of how to live a great life. Without security, there can be no freedom. Without freedom, security has no purpose.

What really happens when we get anxious in a relationship

The way people trade their security and freedom establishes patterns that play powerful roles in the types of relationships they have. When we become insecure, we become anxious.

Then we try to lessen this anxiety by trying several tactics. These tactics may well alleviate anxiety, but they also develop into manoeuvres that we use in our relationships. Over time, these become default positions that we turn to when we feel discomfort.

These manoeuvres, as patterns in relationships, are difficult to alter. They are successful because they help us to keep our shadow away.

One of the clues that indicates you may be "manoeuvring" is that you will have a sense of being entirely justified in your actions. So eminently sensible, justifiable and reasonable do your actions appear to you that no other way seems worth considering.

One of the perplexing things about being human is that the very moment when we feel so assured about our actions and would feel most affronted should someone question the integrity of our motives, is the very moment when we should smell a rat. High dudgeon is the refuge of the scoundrel, and the scoundrel is usually us. When we get on our "high horse", we should start watching ourselves warily. Our motives may be suspect.

This great justifying feeling is hiding something. It's rushing around finding ways to blame someone else while letting ourselves off scot-free. It's protecting us from seeing our own shadow by seeing it only in someone else. In psychological terms this is known as "projection". Projection happens when we take an aspect of ourselves and only see it in other people. This is a nifty trick whereby we make other people responsible for our own issues. If you find this difficult to believe, go and ask someone close to you: "Do I ever make you responsible for issues that I create?" Listen to their response; don't interfere or disagree.

These manoeuvres then become part of the games we play in relationships when we are anxious about security. Unless we wise up to ourselves and see what we are up to, we can be a hazard to other people and a misery to ourselves. We will do almost anything rather than admit to ourselves and to someone else that we care about: "I'm sorry, I'm feeling anxious that I might lose you. I fear at times that I am not good enough."

A. A. Milne wrote about this beautifully:

Piglet sidled up to Pooh from behind. "Pooh?" he whispered.

"Yes, Piglet?"

"Nothing," said Piglet, taking Pooh's hand. "I just wanted to be sure of you."

It's sad, really, that at the very basis of human relationship we all just want to be sure of one another, but we feel too ashamed or scared to admit it. Instead, we cover up our anxieties through tricky games and manoeuvres.

Tricky conversations in relationships

Here are some of the common manoeuvres we use to alleviate anxiety in relationships.

1. **Being reasonable.** This is the number-one, all-time, self-serving delusion: "I am only being reasonable – [the other person] is being completely unreasonable." By portraying the other person as totally off-the-wall, we let ourselves off the hook. This is particularly used when the other person wants more time, closeness and intimacy. We re-label and demean this as "neediness" or "co-dependency".

2. **Protecting ourselves.** "I would like to stop acting this way, but if I did I would be opening myself up to being hurt, attacked." Seeing the other person as threatening may be accurate, but change can only occur when you decide to change yourself first.

3. **Controlling.** "You know what would happen if it was left up to them …" Regarding the other person as defective, incapable or intellectually challenged gives us the justification to control. Of course, people are generally much more able than we give them credit for.

4. **Monstering.** This refers to the habit of turning people into monsters: "She's always complaining." "He's an absolute control freak." The terms "always" and "absolute" are clues that you may be doing this to someone. This actually gives people more power than they really have. It also denies that there is good and bad in everyone.

5. **Resisting an outcome.** This is where it doesn't matter what anyone suggests; the remedies are never good enough. You have become too entangled in the conflict, and will not entertain a solution.

6. **Manipulating.** Manipulating is where we use conniving, weasel acts to get back at the other person. Feuds may never end: we want to add another dose of revenge before calling for the white flag of peace to be flown.

7. **Convincing and persuading.** This is where we see the other person not only as defective, incapable or intellectually challenged, but possibly as deaf as well. "If I say it louder or repeat the message

more, eventually she will be swayed by my logical (and oh-so-reasonable) argument."
8. **Playing "takeaway".** This is where we remove ourselves emotionally and become unavailable to our partner when we are upset with them. "I need space" and "I can't handle this now" are common ploys. If you are going to contribute to a solution, your presence is required.

These manoeuvres all lower intimacy and perpetuate the very patterns that keep tricky relationships alive and well. If you saw your own pattern(s) described above, don't be too harsh on yourself. No amount of guilt ever solved a problem. But shirking your responsibility to construct a positive relationship won't carry the day, either.

Hints for dealing with hurt feelings

Suffering and feeling hurt are emotions none of us seek out. They are also feelings none of us can avoid. We feel hurt because we care. Robots and machines don't feel hurt.

Try to give the issue you are feeling hurt about a score:

0 = not a problem; 100 = devastating.

Now try to give your feeling of hurt about it a score from 0 to 100.
Ask yourself:

- Is this issue as important as I think it is?
- Is this as dire and hurtful as I think it is?
- Is my feeling in line with the importance of this issue or have I blown things out of proportion?
- How can I use these feelings of hurt? What can I learn from this? If this feeling was a messenger standing at my front door, what would the message be?
- Think back to other times of hurt – do they still feel painful or have they faded with time?
- Now that I have a "lemon" (a difficult time in my life), how can I make lemonade? How do I make the best of this hurtful situation?
- Is there nobility in my hurt?
- How can I comfort myself enough so that I can recover?

Now take the following steps to begin recovering:

- Be slow to judge others.
- Act for the good of others.
- Be true to your word – do what you say you will do.
- Avoid gossip and criticism.
- Be kind.

Let's now have a look at what happens when two manoeuvres spark up and create fireworks.

See-saw relationships

> "He was happily married – but his wife wasn't."
>
> Victor Borge

Some relationships work a bit like a see-saw: one person is up while the other is down. Rarely are both at an equal level. These relationships are often based on the idea that "opposites attract".

Some see-saw relationships have an interesting pattern in which one person does all the work to create closeness and intimacy, and the other does all the work to mark out distance and autonomy. One partner may phone, text, leave gifts or do small favours to create warmth in the relationship, while the other sits by impassively or demands their own space.

To the outside observer it can seem that the "distancer" is wanting to get out of the relationship, while the "pursuer" desperately wants the relationship to strengthen. It's not always so simple! These relationships work as two sides of the same coin: one person's role cannot exist without the other person's.

These complementary relationships become tricky when one person always takes over one end of the see-saw (for example, pursuing) while the other always takes the other end (distancing). The people in such a relationship become stuck and limited. This is often accompanied by a trade in impossible deals. This is where one or other partner demands two mutually exclusive behaviours from the other.

Tricky conversations and relationship patterns

For example:

- "I want you to be home more." / "We need to make more money."
- "I wish you would dress better." / "Stop spending so much money."
- "I absolutely trust you." / "Where are you?"
- "I want more freedom." / "You neglect me."
- "I wish you were more outgoing and social." / "Pay more attention to me."

These impossible deals become the axis of the see-saw, and get churned and raked over with terrifying regularity.

Of course, if this were to play out neatly, both people would likely become bored and leave. However, nature has a way of making things interesting. As the pressure builds, people play their usual roles. When tension has reached a critical point, the shadow self lashes out. One person storms off, throws a wobbly, or has a hissy fit – the battle has gone too far. Then both people retreat to their respective lairs, muttering and cursing, to await Round Two. This pattern gets replayed time and time again. With each recurrence, emotional scar tissue builds.

The movement of the see-saw can become rapid in relationships that are flirtatious. A shows interest in B. As soon as B detects interest from A, B distances. A detects a little interest in B, and becomes flirtatious. B responds with interest. A detects interest from B, and distances. It's all very wearing and emotionally draining for both parties.

Things can become especially toxic if A and B both believe they shouldn't let the other know they are interested in them. This is the basis of teenage dating and, for many people, it gets played out throughout their lives. If you are interested in someone, let him or her know, and let them choose what to do about it.

The other main type of see-saw relationship is where one person becomes the persecutor and the other the victim. This can be expressed as:

"I demand that you ..." / "Of course I will."
"You will ..." / "I'll do my best."

"Nice outfit. I can really see what you were trying to do."
Comment from Twist to Daisy in the TV comedy *Spaced*

It is rare for people in tricky relationships to see themselves as persecutors. Mainly, we see ourselves as the browbeaten, misunderstood victim, enduring a persecutor's unrealistic demands.

Viewing yourself solely as a victim disempowers and infantilises you. Blaming everyone else and not taking responsibility will only get you so far in life. Victims get to feel resentment, and treat the other person as if they were an internalised parent. In the workplace, victims can see bosses as withholding, mean and dismissive. In families, victims are rarely acknowledged or loved enough. In romance, they can feel dominated and ruled by a replacement for Mum or Dad. Treating a romantic partner as a replacement parent is a destructive act, and it occurs all too frequently.

In all of these circumstances, victimhood involves a denial of your power as an adult to control your life. And in dire circumstances such as domestic violence, denial of your own power long-term is very unhealthy.

Victims act as if someone is holding a gun to their head; if there isn't a gun at your head, you can't be a victim. Ask yourself, who is holding the gun?

Shifting the distancer–pursuer or the persecutor–victim pattern is a delicate process that should be gradually implemented at a rate you are comfortable with. Always act in accordance with the golden rule: It is better to live to battle another day than to win this particular battle.

The approaches that you may use depend on the type of tricky person you are in a relationship with.

Strategies for coping with tricky people in see-saw relationships

Type of tricky person	Distancer–Pursuer	Persecutor–Victim
Back-stabber	Correct misinformation clearly. Market yourself positively.	Require a time to speak and relate your version of events.
Blamer and Whinger	Is this my problem to solve?	Solve what you can solve but place responsibility where it belongs.

Type of tricky person	Distancer–Pursuer	Persecutor–Victim
Bully and Tyrant	Limit your aims, limit the damage, or consider leaving.	Learn to deflect or consider leaving.
High and Mighty	Stop playing catch-up. Be true to yourself.	Enjoy playing low-brow.
Controller	Slowly increase spontaneity and unpredictability. Help them to see that your independence is not a threat to them.	Don't give in to their demands to know where you are all the time. Don't give them the power to stop your access to particular people.
Competitor	Drop the rope.	Don't enter competitions you are not interested in.
Avoider	Recognise that pursuing is counter-productive. Back off and create clear bottom lines for yourself.	Minimise your reliance on the Avoider. Don't lend them money.
Poor Communicator	Formalise and document communications. Frame them in such a way that if you don't hear back, you will assume agreement.	Don't stand still and tolerate abusive or berating communication. Develop a zero-tolerance approach for insults.

Escalator relationships

In escalator relationships both people take on similar roles that then escalate to a mighty crescendo. These relationships can have a lot of fireworks in them. Tensions rise and rise until they hit the top floor before descending to a calmer level for a time. Whether they are sparking in the penthouse or smouldering in the basement, these relationships are still "escalators". They are often based on an emphasised similarity. For example: "We are like peas in a pod."

The most common type of escalator relationship is typified by arch-rivalry and competitiveness. In these relationships one person generally raises the stakes, the other responds in a similar manner, and before you know it both are going at it hammer and tongs. It's like an escalating arms race with both sides gearing up for a MAD ("mutually assured destruction") outcome.

To the outsider, escalator relationships can look intolerable and toxic. Behind the intensity, however, lies great connectedness.

One lovely couple I worked with treated one another in horrendous ways. She locked him out of the house. He built a bungalow in the front garden and refused to leave. She gave him entrance to the bathroom only. He would sneak into the kitchen and fill the house with food smells he knew she hated. She banned him from the bathroom. He used the front garden as a toilet. And so it went on, with each increasing the battle. Years later I met the couple again. They were happily together and had resolved all differences – for a time ...

Even in relationships that involve sabotage and retaliation, the combatants often won't let others break into the battle. Despite the efforts of third parties to separate them and to mediate, their opponent must be either humiliated or defeated.

It is easy to underestimate the amount of connectedness in these relationships. One couple I knew spent their lives vigorously revealing the limitations of their partner to others. No one who met them could be in doubt that both felt they had married seriously "beneath them", felt they had nothing in common with the other, found the other's ways to be infuriating, and despaired of a life together. Yet when one partner died, the survivor was devastated and died soon after, seemingly unable to face life alone.

In workplaces, one person may loathe another and conduct a smear campaign about their limitations. The hatchet job may become heated and intense. But should one of the people in this tricky relationship depart, there is often a sense of great loss on the part of the other.

When shadow selves collide

In tricky relationships that escalate, the stakes are constantly being either raised or lowered. And underneath this great warfare lies immense attraction. To stand between a great rivalry, or to try to resolve a torrid competition, is to know true futility and powerlessness.

The intensity provided by one person is so captivating and involving that after a time it becomes all-consuming. Each responds in a similar fashion to the other. This is the world of two shadows colliding. If your shadow is locked in a do-or-die battle with someone else's, it is unlikely that you will step back enough to consider developing yourself.

In the slim hope that you may decide to alter a tricky relationship that has the intensity of an arch-rivalry or competition, some strategies are offered at the end of this chapter.

Most people see their relationship as if it were a tennis court, and their responsibilities cover their side of the net only. Whatever is on their side of the net they can take responsibility for and fix. Whatever is on the other side of the net is the other person's doing and is their responsibility to fix.

That sounds reasonable so far, doesn't it? Each person is responsible for their own actions. That sounds fair, doesn't it? Well, there is a glitch in this neat and popular way of viewing relationships: anything that goes wrong in the relationship is seen as coming from the other side of the net.

There is a human tendency to see our actions as good and blameless, and then, when problems occur, to see the other person's actions as self-serving and sneaky.

We can then apportion blame and despair, such as:

- "If only he was more loving …"
- "If only she would be true to me …"
- "If only he would pay me more attention …"
- "If only she would give me some space …"
- "If only he could stop eyeing up other women …"

And on and on it goes. While we may not be able to alter other people's actions, in order to be powerful in relationships we need to try. And in order to make us try, we need to adopt a view of relationships that may seem unfair and unreasonable to you. Act as if you are responsible for the entire tennis court – not just your side of the net, but the other side, the fence, the surroundings, the whole box and dice. In others words, assume responsibility for everything that happens in a relationship. This means you will be asking yourself questions like:

- How do I create that in our relationship?

- How do I act differently to create a different outcome?
- What can I do in the future to improve how we get along?

Now obviously this has its exceptions. I am not suggesting you become a victim and stay with intolerable violence or abuse. What I am saying is that, in most of your relationships, where direct abuse or violence are not occurring, act as if you are the cause, the creator, and at times the solver of anything that happens within that relationship. As delusional as this might sound, it places you in a powerful position to alter and improve your life and the relationships you have with others. Try it.

Strategies for coping with tricky people in escalator relationships

Type of tricky person	Arch-rivals and competitors
Back-stabber	Protect your reputation. Ask them to change. Follow up if necessary.
Blamer and Whinger	Sort out what you are and are not responsible for. Solve what can be solved and move on.
Bully and Tyrant	Observe them closely. Develop security shields and deflection methods. If it endures, leave.
High and Mighty	Enjoy the game! Either try to one-up them in fun or become so low-brow and tasteless that they despair of your uncouth ways.
Controller	See controlling acts as a reflection of sheer anxiety on their part. Give them the illusion of control while you retain your individuality.
Competitor	Don't enter into competitions you don't want. Remember that arch-rivals and competitors can help you to play the game of life even better. Moriarty made Sherlock Holmes a better detective.
Avoider	Pin them down and call the game for what it is.
Poor Communicator	Don't take their balderdash personally. Don't suffer through politeness. Leave boring interactions swiftly.

Chapter 14

How to make a tricky person your best teacher

No one likes being controlled, backstabbed, belittled, tyrannised or made to feel inadequate. On an ongoing basis this can make you feel hurt, even poisoned. Nevertheless, some of our most important lessons come from some of our toughest times.

Tricky people can assist you to become a more developed human being. Even when you are feeling upset or powerless, there is still an opportunity on offer: to grow as a person. No one can take away from you the power to grow as a person.

Unfortunately, most people avoid or leave a relationship involving a tricky person rather than sticking around for long enough to do the work on themselves that will set them up differently for a better future. This is why many people find their patterns around tricky people repeating. There is always another tricky person ready to fill the position if you subconsciously put out a "Vacancy" sign.

Relationships with tricky people may never end. If you up and leave without doing some work on yourself first, their memories will chase you and haunt you. The anxieties they have produced in you will limit you in the future. And demonising tricky people will only make this worse.

The main priority in dealing with tricky people is transformation, not re-location. Staying around at least long enough to fix yourself first gives you greater flexibility in the future. Use the situation to improve yourself. The problem with re-location is that you don't develop new skills, and the problem with not developing new skills is that everywhere you go, you show up.

Transformation involves taking the lesson on offer and changing yourself. You may or may not later on decide to end your relationship with the tricky person, but try to give yourself time to experiment with different ways of relating to them first.

Peter Kramer wisely notes that "depression causes divorce as often as divorce causes depression". It is likely, if you have been coping with a tricky person at work, in love, in your family, or as a friend, that you may find yourself feeling a little (or a lot) depressed. Depression often involves shutting down aspects of your life, turning your focus inwards, being less aware of the present, and being wary of close intimacy.

There is an interesting mirroring effect that occurs. Almost all the tricky people described in this book also shut down parts of their lives, focus inwardly, are not aware of their effects on others, and distance themselves from intimacy.

Again, the lesson that tricky people can teach you is to grow as a person. There are several steps to this.

1. Rediscover who you are

Dealing with tricky people can be wearing and all-consuming. Look for people or areas in your life that you have neglected while your intense interactions with the tricky person have predominated. It is time to regain the territory. If you have been using people in your life as sounding boards or complaints desks about your tricky person, make a promise to stop. Recognise that you may have become a hazard to other people.

Go to every person you have complained to or discussed the issue with and let them know you are beginning to move on. Thank them for their help and let them know you don't want to discuss the tricky person with them again. Your relationship with them is more important than the tricky person.

2. Recapture your spirit

Invite the valued people in your life to do fun things with you. Recognise that you may have been coming across as a bit of a Blamer and Whinger yourself, so understand if people are reticent to begin with. Regardless of whether they initially accept or decline, keep sending invitations. Increase intimacy with the people you care about – love them as much as you can.

3. Nourish and increase your strengths

Take a long, hard look at yourself. What parts of yourself are your strengths? What do people like about you? What makes you a good friend? What do you value about yourself? What parts of yourself have gone "missing in action"? Make a commitment and an action plan to display those very characteristics to the world. Start with people that you feel confident with, and work towards displaying your strengths to the tricky person.

There is a nobility in living by your highest ideals. Nobility and caring can provide an antidote to the shabby behaviour shown by some tricky people.

4. Amplify and market yourself

This involves being more of you. Amplify those aspects of yourself that you value. Act as if you are conducting a public-relations campaign on yourself. Give yourself time to do this: in my work with people, I usually recommend a six-week personal marketing campaign. During this time, attempt to be as close to people as you can.

5. Change yourself first

As much as the behaviour of tricky people can feel unfair, unjust, unwarranted and out of order, it doesn't mean that they will change. Often the person who has the greatest possibility of changing is you.

The behaviour of tricky people may not be likeable, but it is important to recognise that they are trapped and have only a limited repertoire of ways of relating to others. In a fair world, the tricky person would gain insight into their mean and nasty ways, and would either get their comeuppance or come to you apologising and begging for forgiveness. Would you like to place a bet on the likelihood of this happening?

The world is not fair. In a world that is not fair, people don't get what they deserve; they get what they look for. You have probably met people who look for betrayal in others and end up with jealousy; some look for defiance and end up trying to control. Still others look with suspicion and end up with wariness and cautiousness.

Dealing with tricky people can drag us down to their level. We can start seeing the worst motives in other people. De-toxifying yourself from the effect of tricky people means regaining a real-world view of others that allows you to see good intentions in trustworthy people.

Assertiveness is more about the way you view yourself than any specific technique. Assertiveness is about honouring yourself and being fair to others. Once you have made a commitment to treat yourself well, good posture, attitude, firmness of voice, and clarity of purpose will follow.

Become one of "the untouchables". Act like someone who is caring, friendly and likeable, and at the same time is no one's fool. Act as if you are wearing a sign that says, "I don't take crap from anyone, ever." Have a code of conduct and live by it.

6. Expect to feel discomfort

If you have been oppressed or bullied by tricky people for some time, your new act may feel weird and uncomfortable. Changing yourself takes a bit of getting used to, for yourself and for others around you.

Expect that you will be beset by anxious feelings and thoughts of inauthenticity (e.g., "I'm not really as strong as I am pretending to be"). Expect that the new you may take some time to have an effect on the tricky person's behaviour. You have training wheels on for this new role. Persist and remain true to yourself.

Let's increase your discomfort at this stage by asking you to stop seeing the tricky person as a monster. When you view tricky people as evil, you give them power. You assume that they are incapable of changing their ways.

This may be so in some cases, but it lets you off the hook of trying to see positives in very difficult people. Try, for a week or two, to acknowledge the positive aspects of the tricky person's personality.

7. Expect a response from the tricky person

Tricky people have adopted their behaviours because they work for them. Acting in these ways gives them a sense of power and alleviates the anxieties that they feel. Over time their ways have become so successful that they are now a default position for them, so don't expect them to give up their ground easily.

In fact, for a time they may get worse! They may get angrier, sneakier or more controlling. They may try to make you feel mean-spirited for refusing to play their games their way. Some tricky people may be so unused to people not giving in to them that they may burst into tears.

The tricky person has become used to a diet of partial and intermittent reinforcement. This is a powerful addiction whereby your behaviours are rewarded every so often. When you get a whiff of success at irregular intervals, you get hooked on the behaviours that lead to it. Tricky people think that if they persist, you will give in.

Stand still and stand firm. Keep your resolve. Get support from others to help you through this stage.

8. Celebrate

Many of us run away from tricky people. This can cause us to feel shell-shocked and traumatised for long periods of time. Having the courage to stand up to and deal with a tricky person is worth celebrating. Even if you do eventually leave the relationship, you will be in a stronger position in the future.

9. Value intimacy over power

One of the great lessons tricky people can teach us is that coping with anxieties and insecurities by exerting power over others doesn't work long term. It might buy you a short-term advantage, but living your life exerting leverage over others never works out well for long. A great example is one of history's trickiest people: Joseph Stalin. After ruling for decades with an iron fist, subjugating through genocide and fear, Stalin had a stroke. He lay on the floor of his room for days. Probably his life could have been saved. However, his staff were so fearful of disturbing the apparently sleeping leader that they did not enter the room, and he died.

10. Practise having a kind heart

Tricky people can infect you with a feeling of wariness, distrust and suspicion about the motives of others. Take time to look for the best in others and to view them compassionately.

MEMORABLE INSULTS

"He can compress the most words into the smallest of ideas of any man I know."

Abraham Lincoln

"This is not a novel to be tossed aside lightly. It should be thrown with great force."

Dorothy Parker

Author's notes

Page 18: "Strengths and vulnerabilities". This tool has its origins in Native American medicine wheels and has been used in workshops as a useful indication of people's preferred style. It is intended to give readers an insight into their main style, rather than being diagnostic.

Page 61: "More people leave their workplaces because of mistreatment and bullying than for any other reason." "Office bullies" by Linda Childers, *New York Post*, 20 February 2006.

Page 62: "This make-fun-of-the-new-guy/gal culture has resulted in serious injuries and substantial court settlements." This has had widespread news coverage, but for more information see https://www.worksafe.vic.gov.au.

Page 80: "The tricky manager: know-it-all and a total bozo": This was contributed by a person who wishes to remain anonymous. I am very grateful for the use of this profile.

Page 114: "News flash! Working with idiots can kill you!" The source of this story is https://www.iworkwithidiots.com.

Page 127: "There's only room for one in the limelight". This story was contributed by a person who wishes to remain anonymous. I am very grateful to them for allowing me to use it.

Page 136: "The imitating Competitor". This story was contributed by a person who wishes to remain anonymous. I am very grateful to them for allowing me to use it.

Page 153: "When people were surveyed …" A survey conducted by *Time* magazine asked people if there was a 27-hour day what they would do with the additional three hours. Overwhelmingly the answer was spend more time with family or friends.

Page 160: "Managing your board – a guide for bosses and leaders". I am grateful to Lesley Moreschi for this guide.

Page 163: "Great performance appraisals": These comments are from various sources, including the internet.

Page 165: "The shadow self". This famous concept was devised by the great psychologist Carl Jung.

Page 168: "When there is anxiety about a lack of security, we see surges in postnatal depression". See https://www.beyondblue.org.au.

Page 169: A. A. Milne quote: I am grateful to Armistead Maupin for highlighting this quote in his wonderful book *Sure of You*.

Page 172: "See-saw relationships". The concept of see-saw and escalator relationships is adapted from previous work by Gregory Bateson and Michael White.

Page 180: "Peter Kramer wisely notes that 'depression causes divorce as often as divorce causes depression'". Kramer, P. D. (1997). *Should you leave? A psychiatrist explores intimacy and autonomy – and the nature of advice*. Scribner.

Acknowledgements

I am grateful to the thousands of people in workshops as well as therapy sessions who have shared their experiences of difficult people in their lives. Their experiences have informed the categories of tricky people used in this book.

My deepest gratitude as always to my family – Vicki, Lucy and Sam – who tolerated the ranting and ravings of a frustrated author with more patience than I deserve. To all my friends and family who deepened my thoughts through conversation, thank you. You are an inspiration.

References

Brinkman, R., & Kirshner, R. (2003). *Dealing with difficult people: 24 lessons for bringing out the best in everyone.* McGraw-Hill.

Cohen, A. H. (2002). *Why your life sucks and what you can do about it.* Bantam.

Combs, D. (2005). *Worst enemy, best teacher.* New World Library.

Donaldson, W. (2002). *Brewer's rogues, villains and eccentrics: An A–Z of rougish Britons through the ages.* Orion.

Gallway, T. (1975). *The inner game of tennis.* Pan Macmillan.

Greene, R. (1998). *The 48 laws of power.* Penguin.

Kramer, P. D. (1997). *Should you leave? A psychiatrist explores intimacy and autonomy – and the nature of advice.* Scribner.

Machiavelli, N. (1983). *The prince.* Penguin Classics.

McIntyre, M. G. (2005). *Secrets to winning at office politics.* St Martin's Press.

O'Connor, F. (2005). *How to do a great job and go home on time.* Pearson.

Puder-York, M. (2006). *The office survival guide.* McGraw-Hill.

Skynner, R., & Cleese, J. (1993). *Families and how to survive them.* Vermillion.

Index

Abbott, George 75
Alexander the Great 124
Amin, Idi 59
Anderson, Clive 94
Andersson, Dr Dagmar 114
Annie Hall (film) 36
Antoinette, Marie 94
Antony, Mark 27
anxiety, 168–171
Archer, Jeffrey 94
Arlen, Michael 43
Armstrong, Lance 124
Attila the Hun 7
attraction 165
avoiders 109–123

back-stabbers 27–42
Bateson, Gregory 186
Bellow, Saul 136
Biggs, Ronald 109
Bishop, Stephen
Blackadder (tv series) 35
blamers and whingers 43–57
boards 160–161
Borge, Victor 109
Bracknell, Lady 43
Bright John 107
Brooks, Mel 58
Brutus 27
bullies and tyrants 58–73
Bush, George W 138

Caesar, Julius 27, 124
cancel culture 56–57
Casanova 109
Catherine of Aragon 43

Catherine the Great 74
Ceausescu, Nicolae 59
Chamfort, Jean 151
Churchill, Winston 34, 59, 75, 108, 129
Close, Glenn 65
Cobb, Irvin S 42
competitors 124–137
conflict 7–16
controllers and gaslighters 74–93

Count Talleyrand, Charles 149
Coward, Noel 94
councils 160–161
Darrow, Clarence 156
De Gaulle, Charles 75
dying swan 56

Eckermann, Ray 4
empower 15
engage 14
escalator relationships 164, 175–178
Everage, Dame Edna 94

family settings 9–10
Fatal Attraction (film) 65
Fawlty Towers (tv series) 56
fight 12
Flynn, Robert 47
Fosse, Bob 124
freeze and seethe 12

Gabor, Zsa Zsa 74
Gallway, Timothy 135
Gandhi, Mahatma 60
gaslighters *see* controllers and gaslighters
gaslighting 89–91

Genghis Khan 7
glass houses 98
Grace, Dr W G 83
guests 148–149

Hadas, Moses 13
Hadrian 74
'Healer' 20–22, 36–37, 84, 104, 131, 144
Heimel, Cynthia 82
high and mighties 94–108
Hinze, Russ 74
Hitler, Adolf 59, 62
humorous deflection 72–73
hurt feelings 171–172

Iago (Othello) 27
identifying tricky conversations 17–26
identifying tricky people 23–24
imitator, the 136
Independent Schools Victoria 4
inheritances 128–129
Ivan the Terrible 59

Joan of Arc 7, 124
Johnson, Samuel 42
Jones, Thomas 61
Judas (Iscariot) 27
Jung, Carl 186

karma 132
Keating, Paul 73
Kerr, Walter 93
Keynes, Lord
kismet 11
know-it-all 80
koan (Zen) 81–82
Kramer, Peter 180, 186

Lang, Jack 13
Letterman, David 147
Life of Brian (film) 52
limelight 127–128
Lincoln, Abraham 184
Longworth, Alice Roosevelt 27
Louis IV (King) 124
lower the tone 15
Lucan, Lord 109

MacArthur, General Douglas 112
Macbeth, Lady 27
Machiavelli, Niccoló 17
Mao Zedong 74
Marx, Groucho 137, 138
Maugham, Somerset 162
Maupin, Armistead 64
mighties *see* high and mighties
mistakes 55
Milne, A A 169, 186

Napoleon 124, 143
Nixon, Richard M 77

O'Connor, Fergus 160
observe feelings 14
office politics 157–163
office romance 80
O'Rourke, P J 95

Parker, Dorothy 184
Pearson, Maryon 73
performance appraisals 163
Peron, Eva 109
Pol Pot 59
poor communicators 138–149
power 79, 90–92

Reagan, Ronald 138
relationship patterns 164–178
respond with respect 14
RESOLVE 8, 13
Rogers, Carl 167
romantic settings 10–11
Roosevelt, Eleanor 36
rooster, the 99
run away 12

Sartre, Jean-Paul 7
Scarlet Pimpernel 109
security and freedom 167–169
seek understanding 14
see-saw relationships 164, 172–175
shadow selves 165–168, 176–178, 186
Shakespeare (William) 100
Shaw, George Bernard 129
social settings 11
Spaced (tv series) 173

Index

Spanish Inquisition 74
Spofforth, Frederick 83
Spooner, Reverend 138
Stalin, Joseph 74, 183
strengths and vulnerabilities 18–19, 185

Teresa, Mother 165
Thatcher, Margaret 74
treating others 12
tricky conversations 16, 23–26
Truman, Harry 32
Tucker, Forrest 93
Twain, Mark 42, 125, 156
tyrants *see* bullies and tyrants

value-add 15
Vidal, Gore 34, 94, 154
'Visionary' 20, 21

'Warrior' 20, 36–37, 84, 103, 131, 144
Watson, Jimmy 60
Wells, H G 96
West, Mae 93
whingers *see* Blamers and whingers
Wilde, Oscar 94, 108, 137
Wilder, Billy 149
Windsor, Duchess of 94
'Wise One' 20, 22–23, 36–37, 84, 104, 131–132, 144,
White, Michael 186
Wodehouse, P G 45–46
workaholics 122
workplaces 9, 45–46, 61–63, 77, 126–127, 157–163

you 153–156

www.ingramcontent.com/pod-product-compliance
Lightning Source LLC
Chambersburg PA
CBHW011956090526
44590CB00024B/3797